OUR IRBY LEGACY

Curry Brothers Marketing Group LLC
Haymarket VA, 20168

Our Irby Legacy
ISBN 978-0-9847742-9-6 (Soft-bound)
ISBN 978-0-9847742-1-0 (Hardbound)
ISBN 978-0-9847742-2-7 (Laminate)
Copyright 2015 Barbara Irby

Request for information should be addressed to:
Curry Brothers Marketing and Publishing Group
P.O. Box 247
Haymarket, VA 20168

All rights reserved. No part of this publication may be reproduced, stored in a retrieval system, or transmitted in any form or by any means, electronic, mechanical, photocopy, recording, or any other, except for brief quotations in printed reviews, without the prior permission of the publisher.

For Samuel,

"You are the joy that floods my soul"

Mommy

I can do all this through Him who gives me strength.

Philippians 4:13

About the cover…….

Henry Garrett & Mary Gipson-Irby

Henry and Mary Gipson were married on November 27, 1887. To their union was born twelve children, Hannibal, Reece, Lillian, Fred, Anna Eliza, Grace, Mamie, Julian, Blanche, Ulysses, Vernon and Napier. In this text Barbara Irby shares the tremendous legacy of Henry and Mary's son Ulysses and his decedents. Henry was raised and educated by a white couple with the family name of Irby and he assumed their name because of the love and support they showed. During his youthful years he was given away twice. The Irby family educated him, and he was allowed to attend school and worked on their farm. Henry taught night school for adults in both Texas and Oklahoma. The Irby family was deeply religious and active in their church. Additionally, Henry served as Worshipful Master and Recording Secretary as a member of the Prince Hall Masonic Lodge. Mary died November 20, 1940, at the age of 72 years, and Henry died on January 31, 1941, at the age of 77 years.

Generations continue to flow carrying the Irby name, and this book helps amplify the amazing legacy of Henry and Mary. This American family illustrates their overflowing love and pride by sharing their story. The Irby family narrative is a rich heritage and testimony of how powerful God's love really is, and how He continues to bless our seed through the many generations.

ACKNOWLEDGEMENTS

It has been an honor and privilege to work with each of my family members and I truly appreciate your patience, time and effort in providing me with your individual information to make our family history as accurate as possible.

Special thanks to my cousin, Larry Turner and the Irby/Garrett Family Reunion Committee for giving me full permission to use information for my father's parents obtained from the Irby/Garrett Reunion Book 2004. Also thanks to Vivian McCathrion who always had an 'ear to listen' to my thoughts and ideas and keeping me encouraged to complete this project.

To my daughter Marla, my sister Joanne, and my two nieces, NeNe and Nicole, your support helped tremendously when I thought I could not go any further. To my brother Joe, your guidance, support and encouragement to me for following my dreams and making this book possible. Your wisdom is always welcomed because it was you who impressed the importance of documenting our family's history before it was lost forever. Your love and leadership is amazing!

Last but not least, my sincere gratitude to my Publishers, Robert Curry, Jr., and Dr. Gerald D. Curry. Your support and amazing grace to get me to the 'finish line' will never be forgotten. Thanks to Gene Tate for introducing us. You were the right people to put my book on the road to success. For this I am blessed indeed.

Finally, to God be the glory for achieving my dream.

Barbara Jean Irby

TABLE OF CONTENTS

Acknowledgements 6
Know Your Family Medical History...8
Introduction..9
Special Tribute 10
Remembering Mary Sue Looney-Adams 11
Two Determined and Extraordinary Irby Gentlemen 12
Henry Garrett Irby...13
Mary Gipson-Irby..17
Ulysses Grant Irby...19
Mary Cavin Bedell...22
Lillie Mae Bedell-Looney 23
Charles Benjamin Looney, Sr. 24
Edna Looney Irby...25
Ulysses Grant Irby...27
       Lifetime Service Award..34
       Final Resting Place—Ulysses Grant and Edna Looney Irby.....................................40
Ulysses (JR) Irby..41
Robert Lee Irby 75
Joe Bill Irby..91
Barbara Jean Irby...111
Joanne Marie Irby-Ikner..155
About the Author...185

KNOW YOUR FAMILY MEDICAL HISTORY

Some of our Irby/Looney family members have had or have some of the medical conditions listed below:

Aneurysm: A brain aneurysm is a bulge or ballooning in a blood vessel in the brain. It can leak or rupture. A ruptured aneurysm quickly becomes life-threatening and requires prompt medical treatment.

Blood Clots: To reduce your risk of developing blood clots, try these tips:
- Avoid sitting for long periods. If you travel by airplane, walk the aisle periodically. For car trips, stop and walk around frequently.
- After you've had surgery or been on bed rest, the sooner you move, the better.

Cancer: Take charge by making changes such as eating a healthy diet and getting regular screenings.

Diabetes: Have your blood sugar checked regularly.

Heart Attack: is the number one killer of both men and women in the U.S. Knowing the early warning signs of heart attack is critical for prompt recognition and treatment.

High Blood Pressure: You can have high blood pressure (hypertension) for years without any symptoms. Uncontrolled high blood pressure increases your risk of serious health problems, including heart attack and stroke.

Irritable bowel syndrome (IBS): is a common disorder that affects the large intestine (colon). Irritable bowel syndrome commonly causes cramping, abdominal pain, bloating, gas, diarrhea and constipation.

Strokes: Please seek immediate medical assistance. A stroke is a true emergency. The sooner treatment is given, the more likely it is that damage can be minimized. Every moment counts.

SPECIAL NOTE: Some of our family members have had very serious side effects with certain medications, and if you are in doubt ask your local pharmacy and/or doctor. Some side effects could indeed be life-threatening.

YOUR LIFE MATTERS - TAKE CARE OF YOUR HEALTH

INTRODUCTION

Every Family Has a Story
Welcome to Ours

The captivating moments of the Irby Family History has taken me on an unforgettable journey, and that in itself is worth all the trials and setbacks I encountered along the way. It is a project that I took on during the year 2012. Even though there were those days I didn't think it would come to be, here it is, and in my opinion, a first-class masterpiece and definitely an occasion for celebration for all of us Irby's. It is my hope that every page will hold the interest of those who read it, so take your time and learn the worth of our history. Be proud because we Irby's are indeed full of greatness. Through undertaking this enormous task, I became fully aware that FAMILY is indeed very much like branches on a tree. We all grow in different directions, yet our ROOTS remain as one. Finally, despite the unexpected stumbling blocks that occurred, it is because of my faith and trust in God that my dream is now a reality. Through the love, encouragement and support of my family and friends, I wholeheartedly thank you and I am proud to present this Irby Family History Publication.

                                                                        Barbara Jean Irby

SPECIAL TRIBUTE

To our Cousin Rose Mary Clark-Irby
Daughter of Julian Garrett Irby and Estella Mae Irby
July 13, 1922 - June 3, 1985 - Chickasha, OK

Rose died at the age of 63 years, and had great accomplishments in music. So much so, I thought it significant to share her achievements with our family. Rose is the daughter of Julian Garrett and Estella Mae Irby, and Julian is the brother to Ulysses Grant Irby.

At an early age Rose became a Christian and started her musical training. Her degrees in vocal music and music education were earned from the University of Northern Colorado. She began her music teaching career in the Oakland Unified School District and developed outstanding vocal groups for musical composition at the state and local levels. She became the first Vocal Music Teacher in the District to win all suprior music awards at the Solo and Ensemble Festival. Rose was affiliated with the California Bach Society and the Promenade Chorus of Berkeley while serving as the Church organist/conductor for Easter Hill United Methodist in Richmond and North Oakland Baptist Churches. Additionally, she continued post-graduate study at the University of California, Berkeley and worked at the University in developing music curriculum for local Junior High Schools.

In 1976, Rose accepted an invitation from the Federal Government Girl's College of Bida, Nigeria to establish a music department and curriculum. Her efforts continued to proliferate and soon included the involvement of other neighboring colleges. She conducted the First Choral Concert of Niger State with a mass choir of 200 voices in 1977. She was noted as an accomplished jazz pianist and frequently performed in the Bay Area as well as Nigeria. Her musical composition, *Nigeria, Nigeria* was presented to the Nigerian government in 1984, and during that period was only one of seven recent compositions. Her expertise in music curriculum resulted in the completion of two music textbooks.

We the Irby Family
Applaud Rose Mary Clark-Irby for her outstanding contributions in music.

SPECIAL TRIBUTE

This page is dedicated to Mary Sue Looney-Adams

Mary Sue Looney Adams
December 19, 1929 - October 19, 2014
Mary died in Springfield, Missouri at the age of 85

We, the children of Ulysses Grant and Edna Looney Irby dedicate our Irby History Publication to our cherished cousin, Mary Sue Looney Adams for her generous time and efforts in mailing pictures and sharing other valuable information pertaining to our Looney and Bedell family. She is the daughter of Roy T. Looney, and he is the treasured brother to our mother, Edna Looney Irby. Without her support our Looney history would not be as it is. We will miss Mary Sue's gentle and soft sweet voice as well as her kindness, faithfulness and sincere love to our family. Her dedication and commitment in staying in touch through all these 75 plus years is an example of how family ought to be; "together in peace, love and harmony always." We know the Angels are rejoicing because Heaven gained a virtuous woman with high moral standards.

TWO DETERMINED AND EXTRAORDINARY IRBY GENTLEMEN

One dreamed of greatness...

Henry Garrett Irby

Ulysses Grant Irby

One set out on a journey to achieve the possibilities…
We are the substance of their hopes and dreams
We are the fruits of their labor and
We will climb higher and higher
We are the Irby Family

STEPPING STONES TO WHO WE ARE....

Henry Garrett Irby - Chulahoma, Mississippi

August 10, 1863 - January 31, 1941

Son to Reece Garrett and Jane Hardimon-Garrett

and Father to Ulysses Grant Irby

Henry died in Crescent, Oklahoma at the age of 77 years

Race - Mulatto [1]

Henry Garrett Irby was one of five children born to Reece and Jane Garrett. The other four are Howard, Nellie or Ella Carrie and Mary. Henry was raised and educated by a white couple by the name of Irby. He was given away twice. The first time his mother put him on a horse in the saddle in front of her and took him to his new home. They were mean to him and he ran away and went back to his mother. Later, she gave him to the Irby couple.

[1] Mulatto: a person of mixed white and black ancestry—especially a person with one white and one black parent.

(Continued on next page)

They were good to him and he had a happy home with them. They educated him along with another young boy, and both later taught school. The couple lived in town but they owned a farm. The railroad ran through their farm. During the school term, the boys were not permitted to be out of school so they would take them to town. When school was out, they would put them on the train and return to the farm to work. Henry met Mary Gipson and they were married on November 27, 1887. Twelve children were born to this union:

> Hannibal G. Irby (1888-1954)
> Reece G. Irby (1890-1958)
> Lillian Irby-Coit (1892-1956)
> Fred G. Irby (1894-1952)
> Anna Eliza Irby (1896-1896)
> Grace Irby (1897-1968)
> Mamie Laura Irby (1899-1992)
> Julian G. Irby (1901-1993)
> Blanche Esther Irby (1903-1955)
> **Ulysses G. Irby (1906-1988)**
> Vernon G. Irby (1908-1984)
> Napier G. Irby (1910-1912)

In 1904, Henry and Mary moved their family to Crescent, Oklahoma and bought a farm two miles Southwest of Crescent. They built a four bedroom bungalow[2] on it. Henry's mother, Jane Hardimon moved to Oklahoma with them. She was a midwife[3] and she helped people in the community butcher hogs. Jane lived in a small house on the farm near Henry's house until her death.

---

[2] A low house, with a broad front porch, having either no upper floor or upper rooms set in the roof, typically with dormer windows.

[3] A person, typically a woman trained to assist women in childbirth

(Continued on next page)

For several years, Henry would return to Texas to teach school and he would take Reece and Hannibal, (his two oldest brothers) with him. They would find jobs and work during the school term. Shortly after they moved to Oklahoma, Henry returned to Texas and on one occasion witnessed some of the horrors of the Galveston Flood/Hurricane. He also met the woman that had predicted the flood. She was jailed even though her prediction came true. On September 8, 1900, a Category 4 hurricane ripped through Galveston, Texas, killing an estimated 6,000 to 8,000 people. At the time of the 1900 hurricane, Galveston, was filled with vacationers. Sophisticated weather forecasting technology didn't exist at the time, but the United States Weather Bureau issued warnings telling people to move to higher ground. However, these advisories were ignored by many vacationers and residents alike. A 15-foot storm surge flooded the city, which was then situated at less than 9 feet above sea level, and numerous homes and buildings were destroyed.

Henry taught night school for the elderly at the Frazier School in Logan County, Oklahoma. He served as Worshipful Master and the Recording Secretary of the Masonic Lodge in the Zion Community.

Don't worry about anything; instead, pray about everything. Tell God what you need, and thank Him for what he has done.
Philippains 4:6

Mary Gipson-Irby

Weimar, Texas

February 22, 1868 - November 20, 1940

Mary died in Crescent, Oklahoma at the age of 72 years

Mother to Ulysses Grant Irby

Race - Black/Cherokee[4] Indian

The home of Henry and Mary was destroyed by fire on December 17, 1939. Their son, Julian and his family lived there at the time of the fire. Mary suffered a stroke in 1932, and they made their home with three of their daughters, Lillian, Grace and Mamie. The farm was later sold. Henry and Mary were at the home of their daughter, Lillian and her husband Roy P. Coit at the time of their death.

---

[4] Cherokee is a member of an American Indian people of the Southeastern United States, now living on reservations in Oklahoma and North Carolina.

Be content with what you have, for God has said, "never will I leave you; never will I forsake you". So say with confidence, "The Lord is my helper; I will not be afraid".

Hebrews 13: 5-6

Ulysses Grant Irby - Crescent, Oklahoma
March 19, 1906 - June 18, 1988 - Oakland, CA
Son to Henry Garrett and Mary Gipson-Irby
Ulysses died in Oakland, CA at the age of 82 years

In 1930 United States Federal Census report shows Ulysses Grant Irby occupation as a Carpenter. In 1938 a U.S. City Directory states the occupation for Ulysses was a Trucker in Springfield. In 1938 our address was 332 East Lynn, Springfield, Missouri. Mother, Daddy, Junior, Robert, Joe and Barbara lived there. Joanne was not born at that time. Ulysses Grant Irby was educated in the Oklahoma public schools and completed his Apprenticeship in Kansas. He retired from Southern Pacific Railroad Company as a railroad car repairman.

(Continued on next page)

Certified Copy of Original Birth Certificate for Ulysses Grant Irby

Mother and Dad

celebrating 50 years of

Marriage

October 21, 1973 - 3:00 PM

at the Cabana Hyatt House

Palo Alto, CA

Buffet Dinner

ଔ

Mary Cavin-Bedell

November 14, 1851 - September 2, 1920 (Mulatto, White)

Mary died in Springfield, Missouri at the age of 69 years

Race - Mulatto, 3/4 White

Mary is the Maternal Great-Grandmother of Ulysses (Junior) (deceased), Charles Henry (deceased), Robert Lee (deceased), Colleen (deceased), Opal (deceased), Joe, Barbara and Joanne. Mary Cavin married Nathaniel (Nathan) Bedell and they had four children; Julia Bedell, Henry Bedell, Edward (Eddie) Bedell and Lillie Mae Bedell. When Mary died, her funeral services were held at the residence: 1905 East Division at 1:30 pm in the afternoon in Springfield, Missouri. W.P. Campbell was the Undertaker.

Lillie Mae Bedell-Looney

July 8, 1875 - Springfield, Missouri - February 23, 1963

Lillie died in Springfield, Missouri at the age of 88 years

Race - Mulatto

Lillie Mae Bedell Looney is the daughter of Nathaniel Bedell and Mary Cavin-Bedell. Lillie Mae married Charles Benjamin Looney and they had six children:

Roy Thomas Looney - August 5, 1894 - November 1976, Springfield, Missouri
    Roy and Mary had two daughters and five sons

Zelia E. Looney-Smith born about 1895, Springfield, Missouri
    Zelia was married to Landon Smith and they had no offspring

Lena Mae Looney born about 1898, Springfield, Missouri

Matteal Looney-Danforth born about 1900, Springfield, Missouri
    Matteal had one son, Nathaniel Danforth

Edna Looney-Irby - March 7, 1904, Springfield, Missouri - March 21, 1977
    Edna married Ulysses Grant Irby and they had eight children

Charles B. Looney - August 1, 1910, Springfield, Missouri - February 10, 1964
    Charles married Tillie and they had no offspring

Charles Benjamin Looney, Sr.

Springfield, Missouri

May 6, 1872 - September 18, 1929

Charles died in Springfield, Missouri at the age of 57 years

Through all my searches, it is my belief that the above picture is that of Charles Benjamin Looney Sr., husband to Lillie Mae Looney. He is the Father to Roy, Zelia, Lena, Matteal, Charles and Edna. His mother's name was Ann Looney and she was born 1835-1895. His father was Cary Looney, born 1829-1896. Charles Benjamin Looney had two brothers (Seth and Jim), and eight sisters (Railie, Mattie, Lucy, Jamie, Amanda, Sally, Nettie and Lottie).

The 1910 United States Federal Census report stated that Charles Benjamin worked in a wagon factory. The 1920 Census Report stated that Charles Benjamin was a Republican and he could not read or write. The 1920 Census also stated that Charles Benjamin owned his home. His occupation was a Blacksmith during that time. Charles Benjamin Looney passed away at his home on George Street in Springfield, Missouri. His funeral was held at 10:00 am on a Monday morning with Interment at Union Campground Cemetery in Springfield, Missouri.

Edna Looney Irby

Springfield, Missouri

March 7, 1904 - March 21, 1977

Daughter to Charles Benjamin and Lillie Mae Looney

Edna died in Palo Alto, CA at the age of 73 years

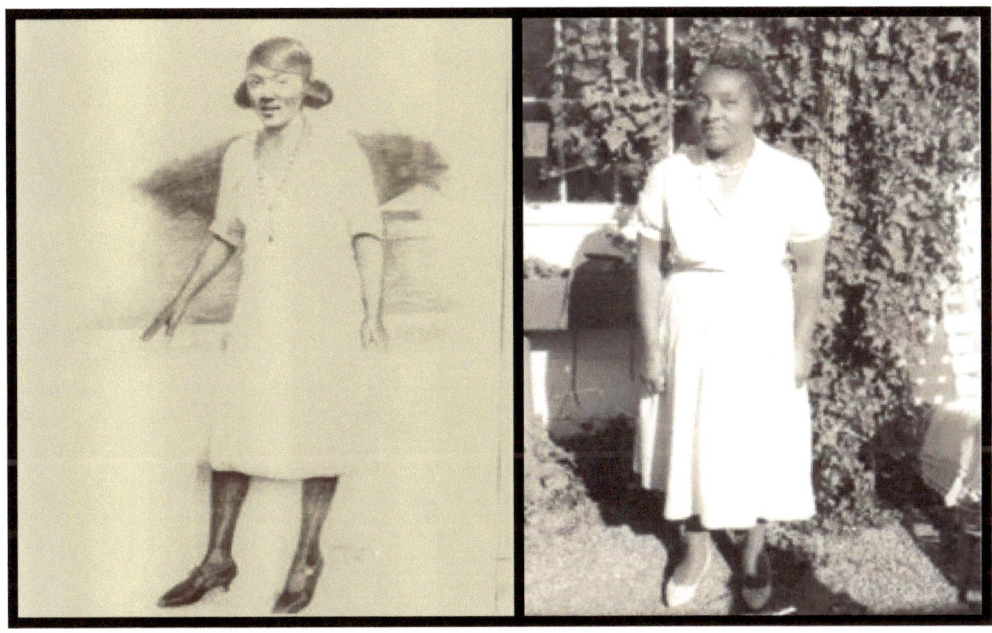

Please refer to page 96, where Joe shares the greatness of our mother, Edna Looney Irby.

Certified Copy of Original Birth Certificate for Edna Looney Irby

(Continued on next page)

Eight children were born to Ulysses Grant and Edna Looney Irby:

Ulysses Irby (JR)

August 30, 1924 Springfield, Missouri - April 29, 2015 Palo Alto, California

Charles Henry Irby

Born about 1927 - Date of death unknown - Topeka, Kansas

I remember my Maternal Grandmother Lillie Looney telling me (Barbara Irby) during one of our family visits to Springfield in late 1940's, that our brother Charles Henry Irby died from Diphtheria.[5] My Grandmother told me she was preparing to give him his medication, and he told her he did not need it, and said "I am going where the angels are" and he passed away shortly thereafter. I have included a picture which I believe to be that of Charles Henry Irby and he lived to be about eight years old. He is pictured with our Aunt Grace Irby, sister to our Father, Ulysses Grant Irby.

---

[5] Diphtheria is an acute, highly contagious bacterial disease causing inflammation of the mucous membranes, formation of a false membrane in the throat that hinders breathing and swallowing, and potentially fatal heart and nerve damage by a bacterial toxin in the blood. It is now rare in developed countries because of immunization.

Certificate of Birth for our sister… Colleen May Irby

The original copy will be given to Marla Colleen Wortz who bears her name.

(Children Continued)

Robert Lee Irby - August 8, 1927 - Topeka, Kansas - June 21, 1991 - San Jose, CA

Colleen May Irby - January 7, 1929 Topeka, Kansas - June 9, 1930

Opal Irby Estimated birth year 1930 - Topeka, Kansas
    Records show Opal may have died before she reached the age of one year.

Joe Bill Irby - August 12, 1935 - Springfield, Missouri

Barbara Jean Irby - June 20, 1938 - Springfield, Missouri

Back in Springfield when I was approximately two or three years old, my Father told me that he took me to the park and while there, I got strangled on something… he thought he was losing me just as he had lost Colleen. He said he grabbed me up by my feet (my head dangling toward the ground) and ran all the way home (barefoot). When he got me in our house, he told me he literally threw me on the sofa, exclaiming loudly "she's dead". He was very distraught and crying believing I had died! God smiled on me because 76 years later, I remain a part of the Irby family.

Joanne Marie Irby - June 12, 1940 - Springfield, Missouri

Praise God for the memories...

...*MORE memories*...

MEMORIES

Unable to identify these two photos, but most likely they are members of our Irby/Looney Family!!

Unknown!

Unknown!

We were all proud when our father, Ulysses Grant Irby received the 'Lifetime Service Award' from the Irby/Garrett Family Reunion Committee.

LIFETIME SERVICE AWARD

This year's recipient of the "Lifetime Service Award" was one of the earliest participants and contributors to this family reunion. His efforts date back to the mid-fifties when the family was gathering in Crescent, Oklahoma. Next was Topeka, Kansas, and finally, here in the Oklahoma City metro area. Throughout all of our family gatherings, this person has always stepped forward with his monetary contributions.

In the early years of this reunion, there were no monetary fees collected from family members to bear the expense of our annual reunion. All collections were done on a voluntary basis. It is here where this person made a huge difference to the survival of our annual family reunion. Every year he would send large sums of money in advance, and also contributed more when he arrived at the reunion, if it was needed to make ends meet.

On years that he could not attend the reunion, he still made sure that his contributions arrived in a timely manner. For his years of contributions and support to the Irby-Garrett Family Reunion, we "posthumously" award Ulysses Irby, Sr., the "Lifetime Service Award."

Ulysses Grant Irby with two of his brothers, Vernon Garrett Irby (1908-1984) and Julian Garrett Irby (1901-1993). This picture was taken shortly after Daddy had put the lawn and sidewalk in at 1036 Laurel Avenue, E. Palo Alto, CA. Everyone would come to see the marvelous work Daddy had done on his home improvements.

Barbara and Joanne during the 1950's with Mother and Daddy in the background. This picture taken at Nicholl Park in Richmond, CA, located at Macdonald Avenue and 33rd Street. Daddy made sure that we were taken and exposed to everything possible. Nicholl Park currently has 21.0 acres of land and is a historical park.

Mother and Dad leaving for church service

Mother and Daddy were avid church goers. When we moved to Palo Alto, California, they attended and became members of University African Methodist Episcopal (AME) Zion church. Mother was an usher until her health prevented her from serving. Daddy was a Trustee and both of them served faithfully and diligently. Daddy took part in a great pageant production at his church—about Adam, Eve and a Serpent. He did a fantastic job. Both Mother and Dad were loved by their church family and whoever the pastor would be, they always found time to come visit us in our home, and especially to bring communion if one of them was ill.

Marla with her Grandfather "Gramps" trying to be a big helper

(Continued on next page)

Mother & Daddy purchased our home at 1036 Laurel Avenue in 1955. The house was moved from another location and placed on the vacant lot at Laurel Avenue, with nothing but dirt, huge rocks and weeds. The front yard looked like picture to the left.

This is what our backyard looked like before Daddy's hard work and determination to turn it into a beautiful landscaped yard, and he made all of us proud. He would come home from his job and work till dark and Saturdays he toiled again, all day stopping only for a quick bite to eat. The picture on the next page is the results of what one man (our Father) did and it is a beautiful home still.

(Continued on next page)

These two pictures are the finishing results of how Daddy toiled away working his fingers to the bone, landscaping with beautiful flowers, and puting in a concrete patio piece by piece to make us all happy.

1036 Laurel Avenue, East Palo Alto

3 Beds | 2 Baths | 1,590 SqFt

This stunning property boasts a bright & open floor plan with a spacious private yard perfect for entreating family & friends. Open floor plan with large living room that flows into the fining area and a dream size master suite. A large open kitchen with granite countertops and breakfast nook, perfect for family or investment.

As shown, our home at 1036 Laurel Avenue, East Palo Alto, California is up for sale or most likely sold by now! When Daddy purchased this home in 1955 for his family, he paid approximately $10,000 for it. Today, 2014 it is selling for $537,000. Wow!

Skylawn Cemetery San Mateo, California

FINAL RESTING PLACE FOR
ULYSSES GRANT IRBY AND EDNA LOONEY IRBY

Take my life, and let it be consecrated, Lord, to Thee,
Take my moments and my day;
Let them flow in ceaseless praise.
To God be the Glory for the life of
Ulysses Grant and Edna Looney Irby

Ulysses Irby

August 30, 1924 - Springfield, Missouri - April 29, 2015

First son and first child born to Ulysses Grant and Edna Looney Irby

Ulysses died in Palo Alto, Califorina at the age of 90 years

I was born in Springfield, Missouri in 1924, and the first child born to Ulysses Grant and Edna Looney Irby. I was nicknamed Junior, because my Dad and I have the same first name. So, let the records show that I am Ulysses Irby, and my Father is Ulysses Grant Irby. I attended Lincoln School in Springfield. In later years, the name was changed to Central and now known as Springfield High School. From 1884 until 1954 Black students in Springfield, Missouri, atttended Lincoln School from grades one through twelve.

(Continued on next page)

My Eighth Grade Class 1938

Our Class Sponsor (teacher) was Mr. Earl Brooks, standing on left side. Sitting on the first row, second from left is 'yours truly' Ulysses Irby. On the same row at the far end, is my cousin, Adolph "Babe" Fulbright. Top row, first on left is another cousin, Leo Bedell. Back in those days Negro children were not afforded the luxury of sports in our all 'colored' school. There were many days when we would look across the street to the "all white" school and watch the white kids playing basketball, football and many other sports that we as Negroes did not have the privilege of playing. As it was said back then, *'THAT IS JUST THE WAY IT WAS'*...

(Continued on next page)

Lincoln as it was in the 1930's

I have one cousin that I have stayed in touch with all these years, (Charlene Fulbright-Weaver-Fisher). Charlene was first a student at Lincoln, and after college she returned and taught high school students during the years 1949-1953. Schools in Springfield were not integrated until 1954, and when it was integrated Lincoln School was closed. In the early 1940's, my Father, decided to relocate from Springfield, Missouri to California. Since I was the oldest child, he took me with him to California. When I was about 17 or 18 years old when we left Springfield, travelling by train. Dad and I stayed with his brother (Julian Garrett Irby/we called him Uncle Doc) in Richmond, California8, so Dad could save enough money to send for the rest of his family. What a privilege to have been raised by two loving and caring parents. At this time, memory does not allow me to share all the things we did together, places we visited, etc, but one thing that will always be in my heart, my Mother and Father loved me unconditionally, and I was richly blessed to be their son.

(Continued on next page)

My first job upon arriving to Richmond, California, I was working at the Kaiser Shipyards (along with my Father and Mother) during World War II—1940-1945. World War II had begun, and the Kaiser Richmond Shipyards, was one of the biggest wartime shipbuilding operations on the West Coast, sprang up on Richmond's South Shoreline in January 1941. Richmond's population increased dramatically from 23,600 in 1940 to over 93,700 in 1943, as tens of thousands of new residents, White and Black, migrated from the economically depressed South and Southwest to work in the shipyards. Much of the new population was housed in temporary structures. Dormitories, demountable houses, and apartments were built; and more than 60,000 people lived in public housing, which included Dad, Mother and their 5 living children.

I have had various other jobs which were: Hunts Cannery during the year 1955 and beyond, Peabody Motors in Oakland, United States Postal Service in Palo Alto, CA, and Great Western Financial Corporation from 1976 to 1989, where I worked for thirteen years as an Appraiser. My job duty was setting values for real estate property. I retired from Great Western in 1989. I have always been a hard and dedicated worker all of my life, starting at approximately the age of 17. I am proud to say that this year (2014) I celebrated my 90th birthday.

Peabody Motors, Oakland, California—look for me on the front row

On April 1, 1949, I married Christia B. Rose. Christia was born to Thomas and Jessie Mae Rose on November 20, 1931, in Lewisville, Arkansas. Her family moved to California when she was about 10 or 11 years old. She became a member of Zion Hill Baptist Church in Richmond upon her arrival to California. She attended Nystrom Elementary School in Richmond for about six months, and then transferred to Roosevelt Junior High and later Richmond Union High School. We lived in San Pablo, California for approximately seven years and moved to Palo Alto approximately 1956/1957.

(Continued on next page)

Chris moved her membership to Jerusalem Baptist Church on Sheridan Street in Palo Alto and has served as an usher, Sunday School teacher and is an ordained Deacon. She has remained a faithful member at Jerusalem for over 50 years. In order to get a decent job, it was important to Chris to get all the job training possible, so she took a business course and basic office training at Palo Alto Adult School, and attended night school at Foothill College, taking a course in accounting. Chris also attended Occupational Industrial Center West (OICW) a non-profit job training and placement center on the Menlo Park-East Palo Alto border, and trained in electronic courses. One of her first jobs was at Johnson and Johnson Company, in Redwood City, CA. She took on seasonal work at Hunt's Cannery for a few years and then her big job opportunity came while at OICW - she was given an application to apply for a job at Lockheed Missiles and Space Company in Sunnyvale, CA. Chris applied and was hired immediately to work on the Assembly Line, and remained in that position for four years. She also did Order Writing for about six months, then took a position in Cost Accounting and later Accounts Payable. Her job titles were Record Investigator and General Accountant. She remained as a General Accountant until her retirement. Chris was a loyal, devoted and dedicated employee at Lockheed for 27 years before her early retirement. Needless to say, I have always been proud of my wife and appreciate her loyalty to our family as well as her love, commitment and devotion to our daughter and four sons.

My life has been fantastic with my wife and children, and there was nothing I would not do for them. Family was important to me and I believe in family gatherings with food and good times. This was a family tradition which I inherited from my Mother and Father.

Christia and I shared our lives together with total love and respect for each other. Our belief and trust in God brought us to a great celebration on April 2, 2014—we celebrated 65 beautiful years together. It was God that brought us together and 'make no mistake' God has kept us together, in good times and bad times. I give total credit to my wife for being steadfast and instilling in us that God's Word would be our family guide.

We enjoyed travelling to various places together and camping at "Thousand Trails" was one of our favorite outings.

Attending our yearly Family Reunion in Oklahoma as often as possible was important to us. When we travelled to our family reunions to spend time with relatives in Oklahoma, we would often leave the reunion for Springfield to visit our Looney family members. We also would then travel on to Lewisville, Arkansas to spend time with Chris' family, and then to Tucson, Arizona. Whenever we could, we would stop in Santa Monica, CA where Chris' cousin Murlie and family lived. One of our special trips was when I took all the grand-daughters camping to Peace Arch Park in Canada. It was an exciting adventure for the girls, and I hope they will always remember how their Grandmother and I enjoyed taking them! The Peace Arch is the world's first monument to peace. Sam Hill a prominent American businessman, conceived the idea of the Arch. Mr. Hill laid a hollow cornerstone within which he placed a hammered steel box made from the steel of a captured slave ship. Inside the box, he placed a piece of the Beaver and the Mayflower. The Arch was fitted with two iron gates, leaving them open to symbolize peace between the two great nations. Peace Arch was dedicated in 1921. Two decades later, on November 7, 1939, the Peace Arch and surrounding lands on the Canadian side became Peace Arch Provincial Park. Words at top of Arch reads: "Brethren Dwelling Together in Unity." I also took my family to Thousand Trails Pio Pico RV Camping Resort in California, located south of San Diego, close to many attractions such as the zoo, SeaWorld and museums. We were twenty minutes from Mexico, and although we didn't go to Mexico, day trips south of the border are not only a possibility but also a great opportunity.

(Continued on next page)

RV members come to Pio Pico for the peace and quiet of nature as well as to escape the day to day rush of the big cities. It is considered a "destination" RV Resort in southern California. I am so happy I was able to take my family on many more wonderful and exciting trips. In my younger years, I enjoyed playing baseball and bowling. Card games were a great past-time for me and family—I always considered myself a 'Champ at Bid Whist' which was a very popular card game among our family members. I spent a lot of time putting picture puzzles together and then aming them. (Some are on display at our home in Las Vegas and Palo Alto). I was also good at word puzzle games. I loved music, and Gospel and Jazz were favorites for both me and Chris. I guess I should have been a comedian because I loved telling jokes and even playing friendly jokes on family and friends. Last but not least, I have never forgotten Chris' birthday or my children's birthday. I loved sending birthday cards to all my family and close friends. Remembering our Wedding Anniversary was easy, because it was April 1st - (April Fools' Day).

Adrian Norris Irby, Sr., Richard Maurice Irby, Shirley Ann Irby-Tomlin, Andre Danneal Irby and Lawrence Christopher Irby, Sr.

My children have been blessed to have Christia B. Irby for their mother. She is a dedicated Christian woman who daily reads and studies her Bible. Her life exemplifies a Godly woman who never once neglected her husband or children and believes totally in 'loving one another' and trusting God for all things. Chris and I are the proud parents of one daughter and four sons.

Shirley Ann Irby-Robertson-Tomlin
August 3, 1949 - Martinez, California
First child born to Ulysses and Christia Irby

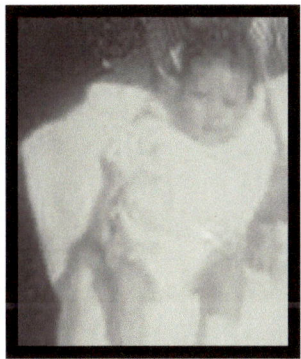  

I married Howard Robertson (now deceased) and one daughter and one son were born to that union, Christia Naomi Robertson and Lorenzo Anthony Robertson. I later married Huling H. Tomlin and we were married for twenty five years before his death on March 16, 1998. One daughter was born to that union, Brooke Rose Irby Tomlin. Hu and I moved to Simi Valley and lived there for eighteen years. We moved to Gilroy, CA in 1988. I went to Moorpark College for my Dietitian Technician degree. Many family members call on me for medical information, and they often refer to me as "Doctor Shirley." I am currently retired.

Anthony Lorenzo Robertson
November 9, 1966 - San Mateo, CA
Son to Howard Robertson (deceased) and Shirley Irby Robertson Tomlin

Anthony is pictured top center with three of his children:
From left to right: son Christian Robertson, daughter Cheyenne Robertson and son Anthony Robertson

Anthony was a student at Simi Valley Royal High School in Simi Valley, CA. When his parents moved to Gilroy, CA, Anthony moved to Palmdale, CA for a few years. He has worked for different agencies as a Collection Agent. Some of his jobs have been located in Sacramento, CA, Las Vegas, NV, Texas, and Colorado. Anthony has always been praised for his outstanding work and professionalism as a Collection Agent. Anthony had the occasion to travel to Africa and worked there as a Collection Agent as well. For a few years, Anthony also drove a Big Rig traveling to various states and cities.

Christia Naomi Robertson

July 25, 1971 - Stanford Hospital - Palo Alto, California

Daughter to Howard Robertson (deceased) and Shirley Irby Robertson Tomlin

My biological parents are Shirley Irby Tomlin & Howard Robertson. My Stepfather since I was one year old was Huling (Hu) Horace Tomlin. My siblings are Anthony Lorenzo Robertson and Brooke Rose Tomlin. I am single, never married, but there is still hope in me. I have no children, but have two nephews that I love and adore and they both bring great joy to my life. I grew up in Simi Valley, CA and graduated K-6th grade at Berlywood Elementary. Then, beginning 7th to 9th grade, I attended Hillside Junior High. My 10th grade was at Royal High School, and 11th grade at Simi High School. I graduated 12th grade when my family moved to Gilroy, CA in 1989 at Gilroy High School.

I then dabbled in various community colleges like Gavilan, De Anza and Cabrillo until I started my eleven year career (now vested) as a Customer Service Cashier at Safeway in 1995. In 2010, I changed companies and am currently at San Jose Water Company as a Customer Service Representative.

For the first time in my life, from 2007 to 2009, I cut away from my mother's 'apron strings' at the ripe old age of 35 -- then had to crawl back and regroup (Thank the Lord for our Parents).

Now successfully living on my own since 2001. "Hands up for all my INDEPENDENT WOMEN!!!" My newest hobby is entering myself in charity sponsored 5k run/walk-a-thons. I am motivated and committed to be healthy and stay active! For my FUTURE self, I would like to get married to my soul mate and travel/dine the world!

I am pictured with my Grandfather above, whom I have great respect, admiration and love. I am proud to be the first Granddaughter for Ulysses and Christia Irby. Although I have no offspring, you will always find me enjoying quality time with my two nephews, Avery and Mason, the sons of my sister Brooke.

Mason and Avery watching the clouds… and enjoying a visit with their Auntie Christia.

Brooke Rose Irby-Tomlin
August 6, 1981 - Granada Hills, California
Daughter to Shirley Ann Irby-Tomlin and Huling H. Tomlin (deceased)

I went to Glenview Elementary School in Gilroy, CA. I received all good marks until commencement of letter grades, which I received Honor Roll and Principal's List. I was promoted to the 6th grade in 1992. I then went to South Valley Jr. High School also in Gilroy CA, and there I was on the track and field team, my events were the 440 relay, the 100 yard dash and the long jump. My longest jump was 17.2 ft. that won me a second place ribbon. I also played on the basketball team and was a starting guard in both 7th and 8th grade. I graduated Junior High in 1994/1995 school year with a 3.98 GPA. I attended Gilroy High School for a short stint where I played basketball and field hockey. I decided to leave my sophomore year to attend an Independent Studies School, where I spent most of my days at home teaching myself and then once a week I went in to take tests and get my homework for the following week. Not the smartest of decisions, but I began working at age 15 and by 17 I was working full time. Although I didn't attend what most would call a 'normal' high school, I did graduate and walked the stage with the graduating class of 2000. I delved a bit too much into the grownup world and workforce, causing me to graduate one year later than I should have, but as they say, better late than never! I graduated high school in school year 1999/2000 with 3.56 GPA.

(Continued on next page)

From my high school years and on I've had many successful and fulfilling jobs in such fields as daycare, where I worked for Parkside Athletic Club (a local gym in Gilroy) for one year. I did Retail Sales at the Premium Outlets in Gilroy (Nine West & Co & Max Studio) for two years; I worked as a Customer Service Associate for Cellular Warehouse selling cell phones and service for Pac Bell which then became AT&T for approximately three years. From there I went to IBM and provided Administrative Support for one and a half years. Then at the age of 20, on June 22, 2002 (one and one-half month shy of my twenty-first birthday) I gave birth to my first son, Avery Robert Tomlin Ricondo. I went back to work when he was just four months old. I was told about a Receptionist's position inside of Abbott Laboratories which was supposed to be temporary covering for a lady on maternity leave. My boss liked me so much, she kept me and I then moved up to work in their Copy/ Production Center and helped maintain copiers, deliver paper and produce manuals that went with the medical devices Abbott Laboratories manufactured.

After about two years, I felt the need for change and left there to dabble in Property Management for a firm by the name of Massingham & Associates located in Campbell CA, which lasted about one and one-half years. During this period of time, is where I met my charming boyfriend Aaron Michael King (2004) and in 2007 we had a son (my second) Mason Aaron King, born on March 2, 2007, and I was 26. I worked at Hospira for an additional seven and one-half years, until they shut the doors of their Morgan Hill facility in 2011. After that, I took some time off to relax and spend time with my boys which lasted a good one and one-half to two years.

(Continued on next page)

Towards the end of my two years as a busy full time homemaker, I volunteered at many school functions and chaperoned several field trips. Interestingly, I happened to be on a field trip with my oldest son's 5th grade class where we toured a company by the name of Intel Corporation in late December 2012, to early January 2013. We were given a tour of the Intel museum and received a history lesson of Intel along with a mini course on circuit boards and how they function in a classroom inside of the museum. I told Avery's classmates, "This is where I want to work when I grow up, kids!" and we all had a good chuckle, well, not even two months later, I saw an opening and applied.

As God's favor would have it, I did find my way into one of the world's most prestigious computer companies, and as a blue badge employee no less (that's the term for regular employees) all on my own merit. I currently provide Administrative Support to the Global Tax & Trade Department at none other than INTEL CORPORATION. All I kept hearing, even to this day is, "Wow you are very lucky to have been hired – coming from the outside, our department rarely seek people who aren't already working for Intel". I simply chuckle to myself and say that's because I'm not lucky –nope, not this kid, I'm blessed! Beginning February 2015, I will have two years of employment at Intel, and believe me, the sky's the limit! This chapter has not closed!

Now, I want my sons to know that my Father, their Grandfather (Huling Horace Tomlin) who was born on June 24, 1923 in Yuma, Arizona and entered into Rest on Monday, March 16, 1998 was a marvelous Dad. He was my great joy each and every day of my life. He shared many family stories with me (even ones that he never told anyone else). I promised myself that one day I would share those same stories with my children, so hang on my dear sons because when you are ready to listen—I will fill your hearts with these same precious stories. I know Dad's Spirit is rejoicing for the life of his two Grandsons, Mason and Avery.

Avery Robert Ricondo Tomlin

June 22, 2002

Son to Brooke-Rose Irby Tomlin

I am 12 years old. When I lived in Gilroy, California I went to Glen View Elementary School where I got many reading awards. In 2nd grade I had a reading level of 4th grade. I was also in Student Council for two years. I've also gotten Student of the Month from Kindergarten to 5th grade. Now I'm in 7th grade. When I moved to San Jose, CA, I went to Castlemont Elementary School for 5th grade, and I was the only one to get the Principals Award .

In 5th grade I also got my book published. It was called My Awesome Day. Now I go to Monroe Middle School. In 6th and 7th grade I got 2 Principals Lists, 2 Honor Rolls, and 2 Maverick Spirit Awards. My hobbies are running, hanging out with my friends and family, and playing video games. In 6th grade I was on the basketball and cross country teams. In October 2014, I ran my first 3 mile race in 31 minutes. On December 6, 2014, I ran 3 miles in 29 minutes.

Mason Aaron King

March 2, 2007

Son to Brooke-Rose Irby Tomlin and Aaron Michael King

I attend Castlemont Elementary School 2012 Kindergarten to present, second grade. I have received "Student of the Month Awards" since I began attending school. My teachers have elected me to aid special-needs classmates because of my patience and helpful skills. I have also been selected from one out of ten second grade readers to read an 'informance' in front of parents, principal and faculty because of my confidence and ability to speak loudly and clearly in public settings. Last but far from least, I always receive high marks and my teachers rave constantly about my helpfulness, eagerness to learn, and my creativity. I am going to always strive to be the best that I can be. My favorite hobby is to draw & color.

Mason & Avery

Adrian Norris Irby, Sr.

November 25, 1950 - San Francisco, Califorina - August 3, 2015

Norris died in Menlo Park, Califorina at the age of 64

First son and second child born to Ulysses and Christia B. Irby

I am the first son born to Ulysses and Christia Irby. I attended elementary school at Garden Oaks in East Palo Alto, CA from 1963 to 1966, then went to Ravenswood High School from 1966 to 1969. My main studies were food service, and I am a fabulous cook, and make the best lasagna this side of Heaven! I served in the United States Army, beginning 1970. I was stationed at Fort Ord, CA and then transferred to Fort Lee, Virginia. I was later transferred to Fort Dix in New Jersey, and sent to Viet Nam from mid 1970 to August 1971, as a 'First Cook' in the Army. In January 1973, I got a job at Palo Alto Unified School District as a Senior Warehouseman.

Shortly after returning from the Army, Diane Marie Bundy and I were married on November 4, 1972. Diane and I are blessed with two remarkable children, Tanisha Lorraine Irby and Adrian Norris Irby, Jr.

Both of them were the love and contentment of their Mother's heart and mine. Diane gave them the warmth and attention that they needed and they are the example of her exceptional parenting. Every day I thank God for them, along with their children and spouses. When they come to visit me, they absolutely light up my life with unspeakable joy—and I love them dearly.

Diane Marie Bundy-Irby
October 17, 1952 - February 1, 2007
Precious Memories of "Lady Di"
God broke our hearts to prove to us that He only takes the best

I will always have fond memories of our family outings, such as trips to Disneyland in Anaheim, CA. Even more exciting was when Pops would take us to his bowling tournaments where we would watch him bowl a perfect game of 300 and his team would win first place for 5 or 6 years in a row. They would present Pops and his team with trophies. Pops has put hundreds and hundreds of puzzles together, and loves watching his San Francisco Giants baseball team. He could cook and his specialty was barbeque ribs and other foods that would hit the spot all the time. He taught me how to cook all kinds of fine foods and that started me cooking in high school and in the US Army. One thing for sure, he loved to buy and drive 'fine' automobiles.

Diane

Diane and Norris

One of the main things both my mother and father taught me was to show RESPECT to all people and most of all to them. They both have been very instrumental in my life and taught me all the important things—being all that I could be—and with that I have passed along to my own kids.

Tanisha Lorraine Irby-Worthy

September 4, 1972 - Redwood City, California

Daughter to Diane Marie and Adrian Norris Irby

After graduating from high school, I went on to college and graduated from McGeorge School of Law, JD, May 2006. After graduating with a Criminal Justice Degree from California State University, Sacramento, I worked for ten years as a probation officer at a family intervention center. In May 2006, I graduated from Law School. I was employed at Sacramento County District Attorney's Office from 2005-2013, then moved on to the California Attorney General's Office in Sacramento, California. I currently handle civil litigations.

I married **Jermain Milton Worthy Sr.,** on April 19, 2002. Jermain is a contractor, and enjoys renovating homes and preserving the beauty of his hometown New Orleans. He is a great father and husband, spending time with family is his joy. Family vacation memories are cherished by us all. We have two sons, Judah Worthy born January 26, 2006 and Jermain Milton Worthy, III, born February 29, 2000.

Jermain Milton Worthy III, - February 29, 2000
Jermain is now a freshman in high school, succeeding both academically and athletically. He played football and started track in January 2015. He runs like a speed train, and all are left in his dust! He is looking forward to college and plans to be an engineer.

Judah Worthy - January 26, 2006
Judah is now in third grade and doing well. He loves to learn and has a great personality. His comic timing is superb, and he is the family protector—safety first! Judah plans to be a firefighter when he grows up.

Adrian Norris Irby, Jr.

May 20, 1977

Son to Adrian Norris Sr., and Diane Marie Bundy-Irby

After graduating high school, I attended and graduated from University of Notre Dame, receiving degrees in Electrical and Mechanical Engineering in 1999. I have been employed at Intel Corporation since year 2000, and I head a team at Intel, working on the latest computer engineering.

I married British Nicole Williams on June 7, 2008. British is Director of Afterschool Programming for the Sacramento City Unified School District. We have two children, Adrian Rashaad Irby born July 6, 2002 and Zoey Asana Irby born March 11, 2009.

(Continued on next page)

Our Children

AR is in the Seventh grade. He really enjoys sports, especially football and basketball. In his free time, he enjoys Legos and video games. He hopes to be a video game designer when he grows up.

Zoey is in Kindergarten. She enjoys reading, playing with Barbies and coloring. At any time, she can be found singing or playing some instrument.

British with AR and Zoey

Zoey enjoying a trip to the snow and showing off her masterpiece of a 'snowman'.

Richard Maurice Irby

December 20, 1951 San Francisco, California - January 27, 2019

Second son and third child born to Ulysses and Christia Irby

Richard died in Woodside, Calfornia at the age of 68 years

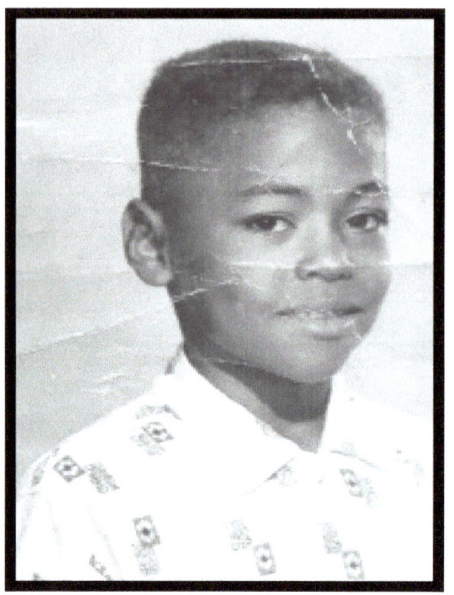

As a child growing up, I enjoyed school and excelled in English and Math as well as other general subjects through high school. After graduating from Ravenswood High School in Palo Alto, CA, I was accepted into Stanford University and remained a student there from about 1973 to 1975, majoring in Economics. Even though I had polio as a child, I was into a variety of sports as a kid. I played Pop Warner Football for two years when I was eleven and twelve years old, and before that I played Farm League Baseball. In high school I continued to play football and received my 'Letter'. I also ran Track and Field where I threw the shot put (an athletic contest in which a very heavy round ball is thrown as far as possible) and disc, receiving first and second place medals. I was also All 'SPAL' (Southern Pacific Athletic League). During that time too, I placed in wrestling for the 110 pound weight class.

I am a member of Jerusalem Baptist Church in Palo Alto, CA, and was baptized at a young age. I am a born-again Christian and enjoy 'walking with the Lord.' In 1985, I started attending Sunday School and entered into Bible Study Fellowship for four years, which helped me when I became Sunday School Superintendent for three years. I love working with small children and teaching them in Sunday School. I am a member of the Men's Chorus since 2001 and enjoy singing songs of praise.

One rewarding trip with my family was going to Canada. It was indeed special and will always bring fond memories of how special my Mother and Father cared about all their children and sacrificed much to take us many places. I moved to Long Beach, CA where I married Cynthia Irby, unfortunately she passed away in 2005. While in Long Beach, I spent time at Travel Trade and Career Institute studying International Trade Shipping via Air and Ocean Goods and Services. I worked in Ocean Import and later moved back to Mountain View, CA and worked in Air Exports until I retired.

I am a computer game wizard and I like foreign cars. Other activities inclued crossword puzzles, and shooting pool. I love gardening too, but most of all I enjoy the good harmony with my siblings, relatives and Mom and Dad. I have no offspring.

                                                    That's All Folks!

Andre Danneal Irby

December 2, 1964 - Kaiser Hospital - Redwood City, California

Third son and fourth child born to Ulysses and Christia Irby

I attended Garden Oaks Junior High school in Palo Alto, CA and graduated from San Carlos High School, located in San Carlos, CA in 1982. I then went on to De Anza and Canada College and during that period, I joined the United States Army Reserve. Since 1989, I have been employed at Men's Warehouse as Manager/Driver. As of 2015, I have been working there for twenty-five years. I love sports, fishing, boating, motorcycle riding and shooting pool.

I thoroughly enjoy spending time with my Mother and Father, as well as my siblings. We are a close knit family and I will always strive to help keep it that way!

Kathy Martinez and I are the proud parents of adorable twin daughters. Kathy graduated from Cal State Hayward in 1993 with a Baccalaureate degree in Computer Science. She then went on to pursue her MBA in Accounting in 2003 from University of Phoenix in San Jose, CA and graduating in 2005. Our daughters, Kiana Leilani Irby and Adriana Lynn Irby were born December 19, 1995. Hope you enjoy their story. We are very proud of both of them. Thanks girls… for making your Mom and Dad proud!

I am Kiana Leilani Irby, born on December 19, 1995. So I am currently 19 years old. I grew up in Newark, CA, and went to school there --1st grade through 12th grade and graduated from Newark Memorial High School in 2014. I have played many sports from soccer, basketball, volleyball, and gymnastics. But soccer was my main and favorite sport of them all. I have played soccer for 8 plus years, basketball for 4 years, volleyball for 1 year, and gymnastics for 7 years. I am currently attending school at College of San Mateo in CA, and hope to transfer in two years to a four year university to get my bachelors degree in Sociology.

I am Adriana Lynn Irby. I am the Granddaughter to Ulysses and Christia Irby, and daughter to Andre Irby and Kathy Martinez. I have a twin sister named Kiana. I was born in San Jose, CA but grew up in Newark, CA. Growing up I did gymnastics as a kid, basketball for a couple of years, then soccer from 10 years old throughout high school. I attended Newark Memorial High School and graduated in Class of 2014. I'm currently attending College of San Mateo with an undecided major and will transfer to a university after I've completed my requirements at San Mateo.

Lawrence Christopher Irby, Sr.
February 27, 1970 - Kaiser Hospital - Redwood City, California
Fourth son and fifth child born to Ulysses and Christia B. Irby

I graduated from Menlo Atherton High School in Atherton, CA in 1988. Graduated University of Pacific in Information Technology. Past Employment: CompuCom Systems, Network Engineer, Building Networks for Silicon Valley's Top 500 Companies. I currently operate my own Real Estate Investment Business. My hobbies include mountain biking, hiking, flying, scuba diving, snorkeling, skiing and traveling.

My wife Cherise and I have three children: Lauren Irby (2 years old) attends Prince of Peace Preschool; Lawrence Irby, Jr (4 years old) attends Prince of Peace Preschool and Jazmine Ferguson (18 years old) attends Logan High School, and she is looking forward to college. Her hobbies include cheer, volleyball, track, and fashion. Cherise is obtaining a Doctorate in Psychology from Argosy University.

Cherise is completing her Practicum hours at John George Psychiatric Hospital and Highland Hospital. Her hobbies include biking, scuba diving, hiking, traveling and she loves being a mother and spending time with her children.

(Continued on next page)

Our Children

Jazmine Ferguson

Lawrence Christopher Irby, Jr.

Lauren Christia Irby and
Lawrence Irby, Jr.

Lauren Christia Irby

Strolling down memory lane...

Precious Memories

It has been lovely being the 'big' brother of my Irby siblings. I was full of jokes and fun… and I don't regret taking the last dinner roll off the table! My mother made the best homemade rolls and there was no way I was going to sit back and let someone else take the last roll. It was fun watching your amazement as I grabbed it "almost out of your hand)!! Well, all kidding aside, I hope these few words will be a reminder that I love my wife, my children, my grandchildren, great-grandchildren including Joanne, Joe and Barbara with all my heart! Although these last few years have slowed me down, I appreciate the total commitment and care my wife Chris has given me during my long illness. There are days when I become confused or frustrated, but she has remained true to our marriage vows— "in sickness and in health". There are no words to say thank you Chris, for your reliable and steadfast loyalty to me. And, finally, thank all of you for keeping our family full of love and being there for each other.

"Pops"—Ulysses Irby (Junior)

Robert Lee Irby

August 8, 1927 - Topeka (Shawnee) Kansas, June 21, 1991 - San Jose, CA

Third son and third child born to Ulysses Grant & Edna Looney Irby

Robert died in San Jose, CA at the age of 64 years

Robert met and married Druella Alex in 1958, and they were married for thirteen years before Druella's death, March 9, 1971 in San Jose, California. Their children are Harold Alex, Sr., Romond Lee Heagler, Sr., Lorraine Marie Irby-Carter, Tonya Carol Irby-Hall, Michael Anthony Irby, and Dwayne Everett Irby.

Robert Lee Irby—back in the 1940's

Robert and Samuel with Bowling League

Druella Alex Irby

November 1, 1931 - Jefferson, Texas   March 9, 1971 - San Jose, CA

Druella died in San Jose, CA at the age of 40 years

D ruella is the beloved daughter to James Howard (born about 1908 in Alabama) and Estherene Howard (born about 1909 in Louisiana).

Precious Memories of our beloved Druella Irby

— Loving and devoted Mother and Wife —

Robert attended school in Topeka, Kansas and Springfield, Missouri. He graduated from High School in Springfield, before coming to California with his parents, Ulysses Grant and Edna Looney Irby in 1942. Shortly after arriving in California, Robert served in the United States Army and on April 5, 1946, he received an Honorable Discharge. His Military decorations and citations included a World War II Victory Medal and Honorable Discharge. He worked various jobs before his employment with Westinghouse in Sunnyvale, CA. He remained at Westinghouse for twenty-three years as a Machinist until he became ill. As a single father for many years, Robert was a hard and dedicated worker, working many long hours to provide for his children. Robert provided both financially and spiritually for his family. His gentleness and kindness remain in the hearts of his children and family still. Young people were important to Robert and many came to depend on him for advice and wisdom. You could always find Robert giving to others, but never asking anything in return. The children and grandchildren of Robert Lee Irby were blessed to have him as their Father, Friend and Confident. Robert joined and was a dedicated member of Charity Christian Methodist Episcopal Church in Union City, CA in 1982. He served faithfully as a Trustee, Steward and Church Treasurer until his illness. Robert was respected and admired by his church family for his honesty and loyalty.

Army of Occupation Medal

(Continued on next page)

Pictured: Robert with Edna (Mother) and Norris, Richard, Christia, Barbara, Shirley, and Joanne

Robert's mother, Edna Looney Irby admired and appreciated him and you could always find her in the kitchen making his favorite dish, "strawberry shortcake" from scratch. She would make a huge pan of it, and if he wasn't there at the time she served it… you can be sure a huge piece was tucked away for him whenever he arrived. Robert was truly loved by both his parents (Ulysses Grant and Edna Irby). Although Robert has gone on to be with the Lord, we continue to miss him in our family gatherings and have fond memories of the great and loving person he was to everyone.

Romond L. Heagler (Irby) Sr.

May 13, 1954 - Portland, Oregon

Second son born to Druella Irby and Robert Lee Irby

Romond married Valerie Stevens on October 1, 1982, in Richmond, CA. They have one son Romond L. Heagler, Jr., born March 23,1983 in Richmond, CA. On December 13, 2014 Romond Jr., and his wife became the proud parents of a beautiful baby daughter Jordyn Calie Heagler, and the first grandchild for Romond and Valerie. Congratulations to the Heagler's and we welcome Jordyn to our Irby family.

Lorraine Marie Irby- Carter

June 22, 1960 - San Jose, California - January 16, 2017

First daughter born to Robert Lee and Druella Irby

Lorraine died at the age of 57 years

Lorraine has one son, Devanar James born August 7, 1980. Lorraine is married to Tommy Carter.

Devanar James

Tonya Carol Irby-Hall
May 5, 1961 - Contra Costa County, California - February 2, 2018
Tonya was born in the car on the way to the hospital
Second daughter born to Robert Lee and Druella Irby
Tonya died in Las Vegas, Nevada at age 57 years

Tonya is married to Craig A. Hall, Sr., and they have one daughter, Lisa Willis born May 5, 1984, and Lisa has one Son, Shaun Pitts born May 25, 2004. Tonya and Craig Sr., also have one son, Craig A. Hall, Jr., born June 24, 1978 and Craig Jr., has no offspring.

Craig and Lisa

Michael Anthony Irby
San Mateo, California - March 25, 1963
Michael is the third son born to Robert Lee and Druella Irby

Michael is married to Juanita and their children are:
Daezella Patrice Irby - November 9, 1986, San Jose, CA
De'Andre Marcell Pitts-Irby - September 5, 1991, San Jose, CA
Dramell Charles Pitts-Irby - December 30, 1996 - Sacramento, CA
Mikiyah Janiece Irby - April 21, 2004, San Jose, CA

Michael and his daughter Mikiyah

Dwayne Everett Irby

March 10, 1967 - San Jose, CA

Dwayne is the fourth son born to Robert Lee and Druella Irby

Dwayne's children
Davonni Irby - May 30, 1987
Davonni has one daughter (Jordan Patterson born July 16, 2008)
Janiece Irby - December 18, 1989

Dwayne's children continued on next page

Jamie Irby - March 14, 2006
Shayla Irby - August 5, 2007

Picture memories speak louder than words…

Memories

Robert Lee Irby with his sisters, Joanne & Barbara

Sister and Brother Moment - Barbara and Robert

Druella, Daddy, Barbara, Uncle Doc, Solomon & Robert

Memories

Michael Irby

Lorraine & her Dad

Dwayne & Michael

Druella & Lorraine

Smiling down on my children… To all my sons, daughters, grandchildren, and great-grandchildren, remember that I am never far away, for when you go bowling, I am there, when you get together for food and fun, I am there. When the sun is shining, or the rain comes, I am there, Every once in a while, I get a quick glimpse of each of you, and I just smile because I am so proud that when I could, I remained committed to being a loving and devoted father and grandfather. Continue to keep our family together and loving always, and never forget how much I loved you.

"Papa-San"
Robert Lee Irby

...but those who hope in the Lord will renew their strength. They will soar on wings like eagles; they will run and not grow weary, they will walk and not faint.

Isaiah 40:31

Joe B. Irby

Springfield, Missouri - August 12, 1935

Fourth son and sixth child born to Ulysses Grant and Edna Looney Irby

This is My Story…

And I wouldn't take nothing for this journey…

(Written in the words of Joe Irby)

Ulysses Grant Irby

Roy T. Looney

The Greatest Man to Walk on Shoe Leather…is my father Ulysses Grant Irby—who toiled, sacrificed and gave his all that we the up and comin' Irby's might have a chance for greatness. Shortly after I was born, my parents bought a house next door to our awesome Maternal Grandmother (Lillie Looney). Everyone on the block that we lived on was related. I spent a lot of time at my Grandmother's home. She taught me how to gather the eggs, and also how to clean out the chicken coop (ugh!!) I was fascinated by all of the things that my Grandmother could do. Grandma would draw fresh water from her 'well' located in the back yard and she would use the water for various tasks around her home, including potable drinking water. She would cook breakfast for me if I came over early enough. I was usually on time because I was spellbound by all the seemingly effortless chores that she performed. I watched her churn butter, can fruits and vegetables, make jelly, jams, and preserves. She had a wood-burning stove and could bake perfect cakes, pies, biscuits, casseroles and fry chicken, fish and anything else that she wanted to cook. She had a large garden (everyone had a garden in those days) and most everything that we ate came from either our gardens or my Uncle Roy and Aunt Mary's farm (including fresh milk and meats). My Grandmother made hand-churned ice cream (I sat on the top of the freezer) while someone older and larger than me turned the crank. Usually at least twice a month, my mother's two sisters (Zelia and Matteal) and our family would have a grand meal at my Grandmother's home.

(Continued on next page)

My Uncle, Roy Thomas Looney (my mother's brother) was also the family barber. He would cut hair on weekends on the porch of his home, that he built on the other side of my Grandmother's home. Uncle Roy and his wife, Aunt Mary had five male children, so there was a lot of barbering on the weekends. It was a lot of fun living so close to my Mother's siblings and cousins and numerous other relatives. Everyone on our street (from the creek to the corner of Rogers and Prospect) was related. Dad had a green thumb, he grew tomatoes, potatoes (white and sweet), corn, string beans, greens, strawberries, watermelons, grapes, onions, rhubarb, and many other vegetables and he raised chickens.

Dad would take me to Joplin, Missouri[1] to the County Fair whenever he could. My father (Ulysses Grant Irby), a man who always looked for ways to give his family all the opportunities that he possibly could, took the extraordinary (and perhaps risky) step to relocate from Springfield, Missouri to Richmond, CA. He knew very little about California; however his brother Julian Garrett Irby (Uncle Doc) had relocated there from Oklahoma. Uncle Doc assured Dad that greater employment opportunities existed in California and public schools were not segregated. Those two factors were very important to Dad. He decided to take my oldest brother Ulysses (JR) and travel by train to California.

Upon being notified of Dad's decision to relocate, Uncle Doc began working on obtaining housing for Dad and JR, but they would stay with Uncle Doc until suitable housing could be acquired. Dad and JR were able to get immediate employment at a Kaiser Shipyard. As soon as Dad had accumulated some additional savings, he then sent for the remainder of his family, our mother Edna, my older brother Robert (now deceased), myself, and my two younger sisters, Barbara and Joanne.

Richmond, CA was new and exciting for me. There was a war going on, but I knew very little about things like that (I was still very young (under 10 years of age), but I knew that there was a lot going on that was unlike anything that I had ever experienced. We had Air Raid Wardens (we also had to have our windows blacked out at night) who would check and make sure that everyone covered their windows with heavy blankets and no light leaked through.

(Continued on next page)

---

[1] Joplin became known for the devastating tornado that struck there in May of 2011. However, the town has a lesser known claim to fame connected to the greatest outlaw couple in American history. Tucked on a quiet street in Joplin, is a 2-story stone apartment house that was once occupied by the infamous crime duo-Bonnie & Clyde.

During the war years, Dad worked at the shipyard almost seven days a week and there was very little time for recreation. After the war was over, Dad returned to the occupation that he had been trained for, a builder of railway cars. Dad finished his apprenticeship as a freight car builder for Atchison, Topeka & Santa Fe Railways System on June 8, 1926 in Topeka, Kansas. His original certificate of completion of apprenticeship currently and proudly is displayed in my home. Dad was a skilled carpenter and eventually retired from the Southern Pacific Railway System. During the late 1940's with the large number of returning military veterans, employment in the Bay Area was not plentiful for unskilled workers. Most of the military veterans that returned reclaimed whatever jobs that were available.

When Dad began working regular hours for Southern Pacific, he would take us on outings to nearby attractions, Golden Gate Park, Fleishhacker Zoo, Playland, riding the cable cars up to Twin Peaks in San Francisco and all the way up to the roundtable where the cable cars would turn around for the return trip

downhill to the rest of the city. We also rode the trolleys to various parts of the city. Dad would take us to the State Fair in Sacramento via train, down to Monterey via train and take the ferry to the Golden Gate Bridge. He would also take me to see African American entertainers, Cab Calloway, Lena Horne, Count Basie, etc. when they would play at theaters in Oakland, CA. He also took me to the first African American college football game.

During the summertime, if Dad was leaving immediately after work and going fishing for Abalone he would take me to work with him. The inside of an Abalone shell is absolutely beautiful. Sometimes we used them as candy dishes or just on display on our coffee table.

(Continued on next page)

Shown in this picture is Dad, JR and myself on an abalone fishing trip. Others shown are co-workers of Dad during mid 1940's. That was an incredible experience.

One time when Dad took me to work with him, he showed me how he was remodeling the interior of passenger cars that were scheduled for racial desegregation.

Although I never really was able to spend a great length of time with my Dad when I became an adult, I will never forget the great childhood experiences that I had with him. I still try to emulate his value system and to be as good a man as he was, both as a father, teacher and friend. He always wanted the best for all of his children and he did all within his power to give us as much opportunity and support that he could.

Dad's character was beyond reproach and no man could go wrong by following the example that he set for his sons. He was more than just a good man; he was a GREAT MAN and a good human being. Dad and equally my GREAT mother Edna Looney Irby, instilled in me the value system that I continue to live by.

The Remarkable Edna Looney Irby
My Mother, My Hero whom I loved dearly

There are not enough words to describe my undying love that I have for my Mother. My Mother (Edna L. Irby) gave birth to me (Joe B. Irby) in Springfield, Missouri. My life was sort of idyllic until sometime soon after Pearl Harbor was attacked. This is a partial story about an amazing woman. A wife who had supreme trust that when her husband, Ulysses left her and their children in Springfield, Missouri and headed for Richmond, CA with the promise of a better life that he would keep his word. She didn't know much about California except that Dad's brother Julian was there and would assist him in getting him settled in, employed, and soon be able to send for his wife and children in Springfield. World War II was going full tilt and there was full employment in Richmond, CA. Dad was employed by Kaiser Shipyards and shortly after Mother's arrival, she too was hired by Kaiser and trained to become a welder/burner. This was at a time when Kaiser was the prime West Coast wartime shipbuilder. The job as a welder in the shipbuilding profession required accuracy and perfection. There was no room for errors because a faulty weld seam could cause a rupture and subsequent water leakage could sink the ship and cargo and crew might be lost. Although at the time, Mother was probably not fully aware that she was part of the EARLY Women's Liberation Movement. Prior to World War II, women were not a significant factor in the workforce, and were usually relegated to service type jobs, such as waitresses, clerks, and receptionists, etc. It was nearly unheard of for a woman to do "Man's Work", especially as a welder/burner. Mother and Dad worked at the shipyards until the war was over and the shipyards closed down. During the time that Mother worked full-time at the shipyard, she also had another full time job. She was an "excellent mother", housekeeper, confidante, friend and caregiver.

(Continued on next page)

It was a sight to behold as her children watched for her to return home from a shift at the shipyard. She would be dressed in leather welding gear (including big leather gloves), welding helmet and even though weary from work, she also always had a big smile for me, her youngest son Joe. If Mother ever had a complaint about anything she never showed any dismay or fear. In retrospect, I am sure she missed being near her Mother and siblings, but she was rock steady and fully embraced to her new home in a strange place. She knew that her sacrifice was for the good of her family. Her younger children, (myself, Barbara and Joanne) did not have to attend segregated schools, ride on the back of the bus, or endure many of the evils of racism. Times were difficult during the war years, what with air-raids, rationing stamps for butter, sugar, coffee, tea, shoes, nylon hose, and many other items. Mother was a good manager of commodities and we always had shoes and a full stomach. She was very supportive of the goals of her family and always offered encouragement, even when reaching them appeared difficult or hopeless. Although my Mother suffered some personal tragedies, she endured them and persevered, never putting her burdens on the backs of others.

Joe & Betty

In 1954 there was still a military draft system in the United States of America, and I had received my notice to report for induction. I elected to volunteer for the Air Force, and after I finished basic and technical training, I returned to Richmond and married the love of my life, the former Betty J. Jackson on August 24, 1954. Betty was born in Jacksonville, Florida on August 6, 1937. We left California shortly afterward and traveled throughout the world for nearly forty years. In addition to living overseas for more than a decade and a half, we also lived in six other States but never returned to California to live as permanent residents.

(Continued on next page)

During our military years, our children attended school in several of the United States and also two foreign countries. We retired in the Fall of 1995, and celebrated 60 years of marriage in August 2014 and now consider Florida our home.

Darrell, Andrea, Charlotte, and Eric

Betty and I are proud parents of four wonderful children. Two sons were born overseas and currently residing in two different states. Our daughters were born in different states and currently reside in Florida. All our children were educated both overseas and the United States. All four children served in the United States Armed Forces. Two were educated at two different United States universities in two different states, receiving Bachelor or Master Degrees. Both are currently successfully employed in their chosen fields. One son is Director/Engineering, the other son is co-owner of a small business. One daughter is a Senior Administrator in the county school system; the other daughter is a Senior Technician for an Optometrist. All four of our children are homeowners and only one of the four is currently married. We have three granddaughters and one grandson.

Charlotte Veronica Irby-Robbins

October 12, 1957

Williams Air Force Base, Chandler, Arizona

Darrell Glenn Irby

September 1, 1959

Naval Station Port Lyautey, Kenitra,
Kingdom of Morocco

Eric Russell Irby
September 27, 1960
Naval Station Port Lyautey, Kenitra, Kingdom of Morocco

Eric is married to Priscilla and they are the proud parents of three awesome daughters.

(Continued on next page)

Priscilla Elizabeth Irby
May 20, 2004
Placerville, California

Erica Rose Irby
April 3, 2007
Beaverton, Oregon

Veronica Catherine Irby
November 27, 2004
Placerville, California

All three of our granddaughters took swimming lessons and are avid swimmers. They love being in the water.

Andrea Denise Irby

September 14, 1964 - Fairchild Air Force Base, Airway Heights, Washington

Andrea has one son.

Derrick Andre' Barber
July 9, 1990
Alexandria, Virginia

Our children and grandchildren are extremely blessed to have their Maternal Grandmother (Ella Jackson) still with us. She resides in our home in Jacksonville. She remains very active and attends church regularly as well as many senior functions. She often travels to California and other states to visit with her other children.

Celebration of 60 years of marriage - Hawaii - 2014

Our Family Faces Reflect our Worth...

My Father and oldest daughter, Charlotte
(picture taken in Oakland, California)

My daughter Charlotte, my brother Robert and Dad.

Memories

Memories

A GOOD SNAPSHOT KEEPS A MOMENT FROM RUNNING AWAY!

Memories

Where oh where could my egg be
-Oops, I'm sitting on it!

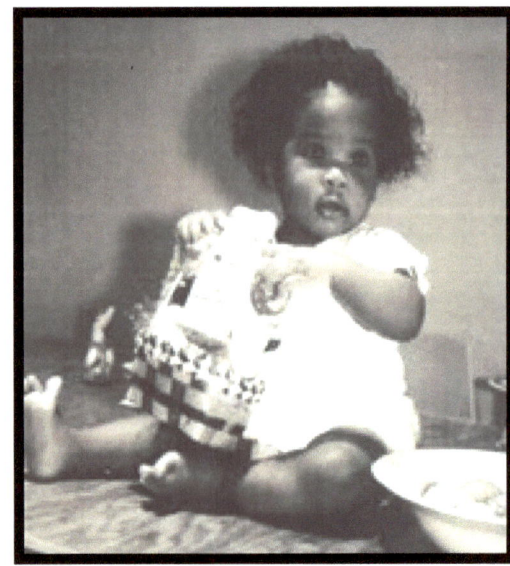

My family and I have embraced life warmly with total respect and love for each other. There are no words to express my thanks and gratitude to my wife, Betty. She has been a "Mighty Force" that has kept us together, and we would not have made it without God and her strength and commitment. We hope our journey through life will inspire each of you today and forever, and never forget that when someone you love becomes a memory, the memory becomes a treasure.

Joe B. Irby

For His anger is but for a moment, His favor is for life; Weeping may endure for a night, But joy comes in the morning.

Psalm 30:5

Barbara Jean Irby

June 20, 1938 - Springfield, Missouri

Third daughter and seventh child born to Ulysses Grant & Edna Looney Irby

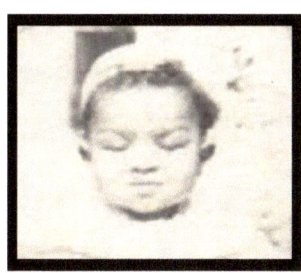

When Ella Fitzgerald was singing *"A-Tisket, A-Tasket"*, and cars were selling for $710.00; not to mention that milk was 50 cent a gallon, gasoline 12 cent a gallon and my brother Joe would run to the corner store and buy bread for 9 cents a loaf in Springfield, Missouri. Back in 1938 letters could be mailed with a 3 cent postage stamp, and to top it off, the federal minimum wage of 25 cent per hour was established. What more could have made headlines in 1938, other than Barbara Jean Irby making her grand entrance into the world and born to the perfect pair of parents, Ulysses Grant and Edna Looney Irby.

The top song in 1938 was *"Love Walked In"*—and I have tried to live my life spreading love wherever God would lead me. And, at this writing, 76 years later, I continue to let my light shine while spreading love and holding tight to the people God has placed in my life.

You will have an opportunity to see why I love my children and grandchildren to the utmost. I will also introduce you to events in my life as I remember it. Some of it was full of joy, but with joy came frustration and disappointments. I made mistakes, made poor choices in relationships, but, no matter the circumstances, I have been able to pick myself up and keep on stepping. God, thus far, has brought me through shining like a beacon.

I pray you will take this opportunity to experience who I am through my story, and perhaps love me even more. So hang on and enjoy, as I share my life over these 76 years. I have included a brief history of important events that may be interesting to the reader!

(Continued on next page)

Amazing History of Springfield, Missouri about 1899 - 1900

During the years that my Great Grandmother (Mary Cavin-Bedell) and my Grandmother (Lillie Mae Bedell-Looney), as well as my Grandfather (Charles Benjamin Looney, Sr.) were alive and living in Springfield, the 1899-1900 outbreak of smallpox in Springfield and the Midwestern United States occurred. From information that I have read, the outbreak was found mainly within the Negro population because racial hatred had already created segregation of the races, and kept them separate. In the minds of some white Springfield residents, that during the outbreak of 1899, the City Council voted to fence the "colored burial ground" from the white section. A panic arose and Negro Springfield residents were not allowed to walk the same road as whites to honor their dead. Negroes had to carry their dead through railroad tracks that was full of weeds and overgrown fields just to reach their resting place. Even with all that, they had to enter the cemetery through the back gate!

Brief History of Richmond, California Shipyards

Henry J. Kaiser established his first Richmond shipyard, beginning in December, 1940. More than 747 vessels were built in the four Richmond Kaiser Shipyards during World War II. Let it be known, here, now and forever more… that my Father, Ulysses Grant and my Mother, Edna Looney Irby, were a part of this important endeavor. By 1944 it was only taking a little over two weeks to assemble a Liberty ship by standard methods. During World War II, thousands of men and women worked in very hazardous jobs. Thousands of people came from all over the United States to Richmond, CA in three short years. For many of them, this was the first time they worked and earned money. Women and minorities entered the workforce in areas previously denied to them. During this amazing time in history, Daddy chose to bring and raise his five living children during the early 1940's to California, so that we might have an opportunity to better things in life (education and jobs).

Daddy standing in front of our house in early 1940's.

(Continued on next page)

BIRDS EYE VIEW: Photo above was taken in 1943/1944 and represents what our projects looked like when we first moved to Richmond, California from Springfield, Missouri. We were located somewhere in the upper middle area of this picture. The address I remember most during our arrival to California is 700 South 24th Street, Apt. 2-E, Richmond, CA. Our place of residence was better known as the 'projects'. Our home was very small then, and included a living room and kitchen area combined, a small bathroom with paper thin walls and two extremely small bedrooms. Joanne, Joe and myself shared a bedroom together. The kitchen itself was small (not large enough for two people to be in at same time) and had a few shelves for our dishes, a kitchen counter space for washing dishes, etc. and a small stove. Our ice-box was sitting in the living room area. We would always look out for the 'iceman' who delivered ice so our food would not spoil. Daddy bought Mother a Maytag ringer type washing machine while we were living in Richmond. Joanne and I loved to help Mother with the washing. Joanne would put the clothes through the ringer and I would be on the back side, catching the clothes to put in a basket, so our Mother could hang outside on the clothes line to dry. Once part of Joanne's hand was coming through the wringer, so that ended our assisting Mother with the washing, while Joanne being the youngest, I was scolded big time!

(Continued on next page)

Regardless of our crowded conditions, we survived as a 'close knit' family unit, and we loved and cared for each other unconditionally. We may not have gotten everything we wanted, but rest assured, we had everything we needed. During the late 1940's we got our first telephone, which was a 2-party line. When we picked up the phone and someone else was talking, we were taught to hang up and try later and not listen in on someone else's conversation, "oh well". Radio was a big thing back then. Our whole project building would 'shake, rattle and roll' when Joe Louis would knock out someone or just win a fight. Now, the real excitement came when Daddy bought us our first television (with rabbit ears) so we could get decent reception and one of the first programs we (as kids) watched was *"It's Howdy Doody Time"* and then *Laurel and Hardy* came on. Daddy also bought us a piano in the late 1940's and Joanne and I were able to take piano lessons. Mother could play just about anything you could name. It was always so heartwarming to hear her play old gospel or spiritual songs. She had an awesome gift and although she 'played by ear'… she was fantastic. When birthdays came around she would begin playing "happy birthday". There was absolutely nothing she could not play and oh how beautiful it sounded as she ran her fingers across those piano keys.

My mother was soft spoken and gentle in her words, but firm in her beliefs. Daddy was a man of few words, but when he spoke, he spoke with certainty and I listened to his instructions and advice with great respect. They raised all their children as equals and always aware of our specific needs. I thank God for how they both raised me, because their valuable principles proved to be the greatest 'road map' for raising my four children. What I am today, I owe to God and my parents. My special times were when I had moved out on my own, but came back home (frequently) to visit and spend time with them. When they would open the door and see me and my children, they both always expressed gladness that included warm smiles; and that made me "leap for joy". Usually, there was always good food prepared, good laughs, but more importantly the satisfaction and enjoyment of just being 'home' with them.

Oh my dearest Mother. I miss you and Daddy tremendously! One thing I will never forget is when I worked at Philco Ford Company in Palo Alto, CA during the 1960's. I began saving "Fifty Dollar" US Savings Bonds and they were especially for my Mother.

(Continued on next page)

What a delight on her face, when she would get the bonds ($37.50) each (in her name only). She didn't give them a chance to mature, but the sunshine those bonds added to her days was absolutely what God intended. Mother was very grateful and loved to take the commuter train to Hillsdale Shopping Center in Hillsdale, CA to shop. I thank God that I did that for her. After about 10 years living in the Richmond projects, my Father was very determined to give us the best of the best, and in 1954/55 we began "moving on up" and reaped the harvest of Daddy's hard work. Moving to 1036 Laurel Avenue, Palo Alto, CA was like heaven! Joanne and I shared a bedroom and Mother and Daddy had their own bedroom. We had a very large kitchen, living room and dining room area, with one nice size bathroom with a bath tub. Wow, we had definitely "moved on up" in 1955.

Pictured above shows what the automobiles looked like back in 1940's.

(Continued on next page)

School Days

Since I was about five years old upon our arrival to California, the first school I attended was Nystrom Elementary School in Richmond. Pictured below is my 4th or 5th Grade Class where my teacher was Mrs. Nunn, can you find me?

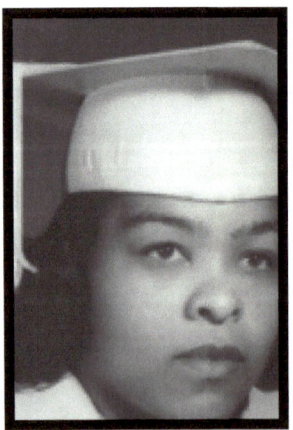

Class of 1956
Menlo Atherton High

After elementary school, I went to Longfellow Junior High. While still a Junior High school student, I received an award as "Champion Typist", for typing 90 words per minute (with no errors) on a manual typewriter in the early 1950's. The article and my pictures appeared in the Richmond Times city newspaper announcing my achievement! We were indeed blessed to attend integrated schools. While in Junior High and High School, I participated in many sports; basketball, volleyball, archery, tennis and swimming. When I graduated High School in 1956 from Menlo Atherton in the city of Atherton, California, my graduation class was about 500 students and I was one of three Black students (two Black females and one Black male) in my graduating class.

(Continued on next page)

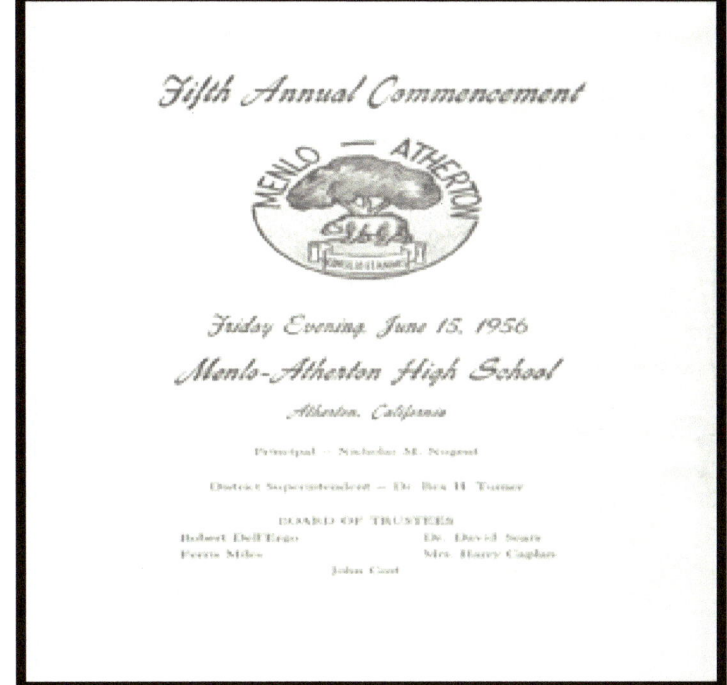

During the 1960's I attended both Foothill College in Los Altos, California, and De Anza College in Cupertino California, taking English and business courses. I began my working career with the following companies, Pacific Bell Telephone in San Francisco, Pan American Airlines at San Francisco Airport, Varian Associates and Philco Ford both in Palo Alto. I held a "Top Secret Clearance" for both Varian and Philco. In the early 1960's I was hired at Stanford University as a typist and proofreader in the Applied Electronics Lab. Later I took a job as secretary to Prof. Oscar Buneman in the Electronics Research Lab. During my early years at Stanford, I was selected along with 99 other secretaries, for a round trip United Airlines flight from San Francisco to Seattle, Washington with a fabulous dinner aboard the flight. This was an appreciation award for the "100 most outstanding secretaries" during the early 1960's. I also worked as Secretary to Dave Fulton in the General Secretaries Office, where I was selected by Trustee, John Gardner to a function in Southern California to promote the $300 Million Dollar Campaign for Stanford University.

(Continued on next page)

List of Graduating Class - 1956

I left Stanford for a brief time and moved to Oakland, CA and took jobs at Cutter Laboratories as secretary to 12 engineers, University of California Berkeley as a Technical Typist, secretary to six counselors at Oakland Technical High School in Oakland, CA; and I worked as secretary to the Vice Principal at Woodrow Wilson Junior High School in Oakland.

I returned to Stanford University in February 1974, as a Statistical Typist in the Statistics Department. For another 13 years, I worked for Residential Education and was Office Manager at Lagunita Court Residence Dorm and was often referred to as "Mom" by many students. One Resident Fellow at Lagunita, (Orrin "Rob" Robinson) wrote upon my retirement from Stanford. "Barbara was always there for me and for the dorm, Lagunita and the people in it were like another family to her, and she treated us like family, not just another job. For many of the students in the dorm, she was something of a mother figure, a person to go to for sympathy and advice even before the Resident Associate or the Resident Fellow. Often enough, my own sons saw her that way. When I left the dorm, Barbara was one of the main things I missed. Her departure from Stanford will leave a lot more people feeling that way. I wish her great happiness and an exciting future life in Las Vegas".

After leaving Lagunita, around 1989, I took a position at Escondido Village as Apartment Assignment Coordinator for approximately 3,000 residents (which included students, spouses and their children). After working for three years at Escondido Village, I was approached and asked to consider a secretarial position in the African and Afro-American Studies Department; where I would work for Prof. Horace Porter who was Chairman of the Afro-American Department as well as an English Professor. Needless to say, I applied and was hired immediately. Prof. Porter always spoke highly of me and to this day, I remain friends with him and his family. The last job I held at Stanford before retiring, was working for Herb Fong in Facilities Operations. I worked for him approximately eight years. I served as Personnel Coordinator as well as Office Manager. When I retired July 24, 2001, Mr. Fong wrote in my 'evaluation' that "Barbara takes real ownership and responsibility for her position. She is conscientious, reliable, dedicated, accurate, timely and responsive. Her personality fits well with others and the general public. She established a sense of family and commitment to the job that is evident in her actions and work. Her attendance is excellent and there have been very few administrators that I have worked with that are as competent, professional and such a pleasure to work with.

(Continued on next page)

I have received numerous 'outstanding student service awards' from the Stanford Community. I served as Youth Director and Young Adult Advisor in Salinas, CA where I attended St. James C.M.E. Church. I have served as Sunday School teacher for many years as well as typing and compiling church bulletins. I have written and produced three "Live Christmas Nativity" pageants with live sheep and other animals to set the scene; which took place in Salinas, San Jose and Fremont, CA. I also coordinated other plays and pageants for Children Shelters in San Jose area. I coordinated other plays and did volunteer work for 'Shade Tree, a women and children shelter and St Rose Hospital, both in Las Vegas, NV. Wherever God would lead me, with a gracious and willing heart, I would go and assist others.

In sharing my employment history with family and friends, I hope someone will be inspired by my perseverance and never give up. I give credit to my Father, Ulysses Grant Irby, because I took his advice long years ago, and I promised him I would remain steadfast, allowing no one to run me away from a job. Even when difficulty came I remained strong and determined, even when I was faced with adversity. I stayed committed and dedicated, keeping dear to my spirit what my father taught me, and praise God, I retired with a total of 46 long prosperous years of employment and 32 of those years were at Stanford University. I know Daddy would have been proud of my accomplishments.

I am a proud Mother, Grandmother, Great-Grandmother with one marvelous son, three awesome daughters, five special Grandsons and one Great-Grandson. Praises to God, on January 7, 2015, I was blessed with my first Great-Granddaughter Richelle Barbara Myers. My second great granddaughter was born August 24, 2018, Ava Marielle Robinson. Hooray, our family continues to grow!

I am included with 3 of my children — Monica, Michelle and Samuel.

Marla

My five Grandsons: Marchel, Durell, Richard, Andre & Ryan

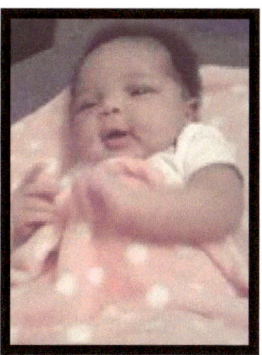

My first Great-Granddaughter Richelle Barbara Myers

"My second great granddaughter Ava Marielle Robinson

My Great-Grandson Quincy Rafael Smith

Monica Ann Darden-Batchelor

January 1, 1957 - San Francisco, California

First daughter and child born to Barbara Jean Irby and Sam Darden, Jr.

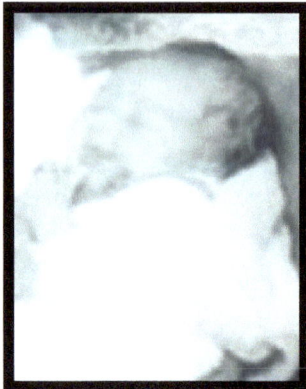
A few days old

Four months old

Two years old - 1959

I was born in San Francisco, California on January 1, and the very first baby born in San Francisco 1957. I weighed 6 pounds, 12 ounces and was born twenty-two minutes into the new year. My mother was expecting to be showered with gifts (because that is what normally happens for the first baby born of each new year). However after it was discovered my mother was Black, they unfortunately decided there would be no gifts, but one shoe store in Palo Alto, California, gave me my first pair of walking shoes! It was amazing how one nurse told my mother, "oh they decided to not give gifts this year". In 1958, my mother took me by train to Springfield, Missouri, so my Maternal GreatGrandmother, Lillie Looney could meet me.

Monica and Great-Grandmother Looney

(Continued on next page)

I went to Elementary school in East Palo Alto, CA and attended Brentwood Elementary School. Above is my Kindergarten picture, Spring of 1963, I was six years old. I also attended BeBe Patton Christian Academy in Oakland, CA. I graduated from Skyline High in 1975 also located in Oakland. I have two wonderful sons and they are the joy of my life. At Skyline, I met Richard Doron Myers (deceased) and we have one son together, Richard Doron Myers, Jr. Richard was born November 12, 1975. My second son, Andre Marcel Allen was born May 10, 1983. His father is Ray Allen who resides in Oakland, CA. Andre is not married and has no offspring.

I moved to Anchorage, Alaska in 1989, where my Paternal Grandmother (Madie Watts) and father lived. While in Alaska, I met and married Eugene Christopher Batchelor and although poor health has divided us, we remain married. I returned to Oakland, CA in 2009.

My Mother, Barbara Jean Irby, was always there for me and my sons. I love her very much and thank her for all that she did for both Richard and Andre. Not only do I thank my mother, but also my sisters and brother have been very helpful to me and my sons. Thank you Samuel, Michelle and Marla.

Richard Doron Myers, Jr.

November 12, 1975 - Kaiser Hospital, Redwood City, CA

First son and first child born to Monica Anne Darden and Richard Doron Myers, Sr.

During my early years, my Grandmother (Barbara) and my Uncle Sam shared in raising me and helped me to be the man I am today. My Aunt Michelle and Aunt Marla also took great care of me as well. Later, I lived with my Father, Richard Doron Myers in Antioch and I graduated Antioch Senior High School in Antioch, CA on June 18, 1993.

1981-1982 First Grade
6 Years old

Approx. 2012

My Father and I spent a great deal of time together, and we both had a great love for fishing. Even though my Father passed away, I still carry on our tradition of "catching fish"—but I throw them back! I have many fond memories of the years that my Grandmother "Mom" (Barbara) raised me. My Grandmother is the greatest and I love her very much. She always took me to Sunday School and Church and many other wonderful places. I remember when I had to learn and recite "Martin Luther King's speech, "I Have a Dream" Last but not least, I am grateful for the bonding my mother (Monica) and I have developed. Thank you Mom for being there for me. I worked along side of my father for years. He had his own Janitorial Service and I learned a great deal from him. I continue in that trade of business and can fix most household items, as well as landscaping work. I am a great house painter (inside and out) and take great pride in the work I do. Looking for a handyman, please give me a call!

On Wednesday, January 7, 2015, at 2:49 PM, I became proud Father to a beautiful baby daughter—Richelle Barbara Myers—weighing in at 9 pounds 1.8 ounces and 21 inches long. Her mother (Shantee Wilson) and I are excited about this bundle of joy added to our lives.

Andre Marcel Allen

May 10, 1983 - Kaiser Hospital, Hayward, CA

Second son and second child born to Monica Anne Darden and first son to Ray Allen

Kindergarten

14 years old

I graduated from Oakland Technical High School in June 2002 in Oakland, CA. I attended Delta College in Stockton, CA in August 2002 and made the basketball team. I later attended Laney College in January 2003 and played on the basketball team for Laney College. I had an opportunity to also play on a Men's Private League. I am employed at Grocery Outlet Stores in Oakland and also work as a Security Guard.

While I was growing up, every Thanksgiving I would spend with my Grandmother (Barbara) and family. During those years, I was a very picky eater, no turkey dinner for me, just 'hot dogs", and Grandma made sure hot dogs was a part of our Thanksgiving Menu. She always made sure I was included in every family event possible and I have taken great pride in keeping in touch with her throughout my life and letting her know how much I love her.

Memories

Samuel Darden III

January 11, 1959 - San Mateo, California - July 1, 2017

First son and second child born to Barbara Jean Irby and Sam Darden, Jr.

Samuel died in Freemont, California at age 58 years

I am blessed to have grown up in a loving family environment. My Mom (Barbara Jean Irby) has been the Best Mom you could ever ask for. My Mom has been by my side from the time I was born, to the present. She has supported me through all the good times, and also the times I have struggled. For that, I am truly grateful and love her with all my heart.

When I had to have both my hips replaced, who do you think was by my side and nursed me back to recovery --that's right, my Mom. Thank you Mom! My sister, Marla was also right there. Thank you Marla.

I am also grateful for my Father (Solomon Wortz) who also helped raise me to be a good person and have good morals when I was just a little boy. I realize now, more than ever what a great man he is and still is to have helped my Mom raise four children. Thank you Daddy.

As I grew older, I can remember my Mom helping me get my first three jobs. First, there was the 'Circle Star Theater' in San Carlos, CA. My Mom was an usher at the Circle Star, and helped me get my first job as a door person. It was really fun working there. Second, my Mom helped me get a job at Moffett Field Commissary bagging groceries for tips. The tips were really good back then. Sometimes I would make $60 to $70 dollars in a day.

That was very good money in the mid 1970's. The third job my Mom helped me get was in 1975. She was shopping at Lucky Stores in San Jose, CA, and told the assistant manager she had a son that knew how to bag groceries. The manager said "send him in for an interview" and the rest is history. Although I had a passion for the court system and being a court reporter piqued my interested, I chose to work in the retail grocery business. I became an 'Apprentice Butcher' in 1977 and began my career. I was promoted to a Meat Manager at the age of 21 and worked for Lucky Stores for over 35 years. I retired from Lucky Store in 2010.

Bea Sullivan

In 1987, I married Michele Terese Wilkinson and we were blessed to have a wonderful and beautiful son, Ryan Andrew Darden, born March 30, 1993 at Kaiser Hospital, San Jose, CA. Ryan is the love of my life, and I will always support him as my Mom supported me. Ryan's mother (Michele) was born on January 4, 1967, her birthplace is Koeppern, West Germany. Michele's birth mother is Heidrum Remmele. Bea Sullivan and her husband George went to Germany and adopted Michele when she was three months old. Bea Sullivan has been the greatest Mother-in-law in fact she is an amazing best friend, and I am grateful for her staying in touch and being in my life all these years. Bea, I will love you always. Michele's birth mother lives in Freiburg/BRG Germany. Unfortunately, Michele's precious life was cut short when she passed away on July 28, 2010 at the tender age of 43. God bless her and God bless her soul. Ryan is also blessed to have one sister and one brother (Kyle and Wesley Martin). They both love Ryan and proud that he is their big brother. I thank God for our family connection that is full of love. Both Kyle and Wesley are dear to my heart as well and there is nothing I wouldn't do for them. They call me "Daddy Sam" and that always makes me smile!

(Continued on next page)

Elizabeth Ann Tiapon

I am also grateful for Elizabeth Ann Tiapon and her family for coming into my life. Elizabeth has been an Angel sent from Heaven. She has helped me raise my only son, Ryan for over 19 years. For her loyalty and commitment, I am thankful and grateful.

My hobbies are bowling, chess and basketball. As for my bowling highlights, I just love bowling and watching people bowl. I also love coaching and watching people progress and succeed at this sport. Although I have bowled twenty-one 300 games and four 800 series, my bowling goals are to challenge myself to be the best I can be and to help others be the best they can be.

Things that I don't like are bullies, disrespectful people and people that try and take advantage of others. Things I do like, are good people who love to help others succeed. Getting back to Ryan, I have always been proud of his academic achievements and his commitment to excellence in all he has set out to do. Thank you Ryan for making your Dad proud. One of his report cards from his Junior High School Days is on the next page.

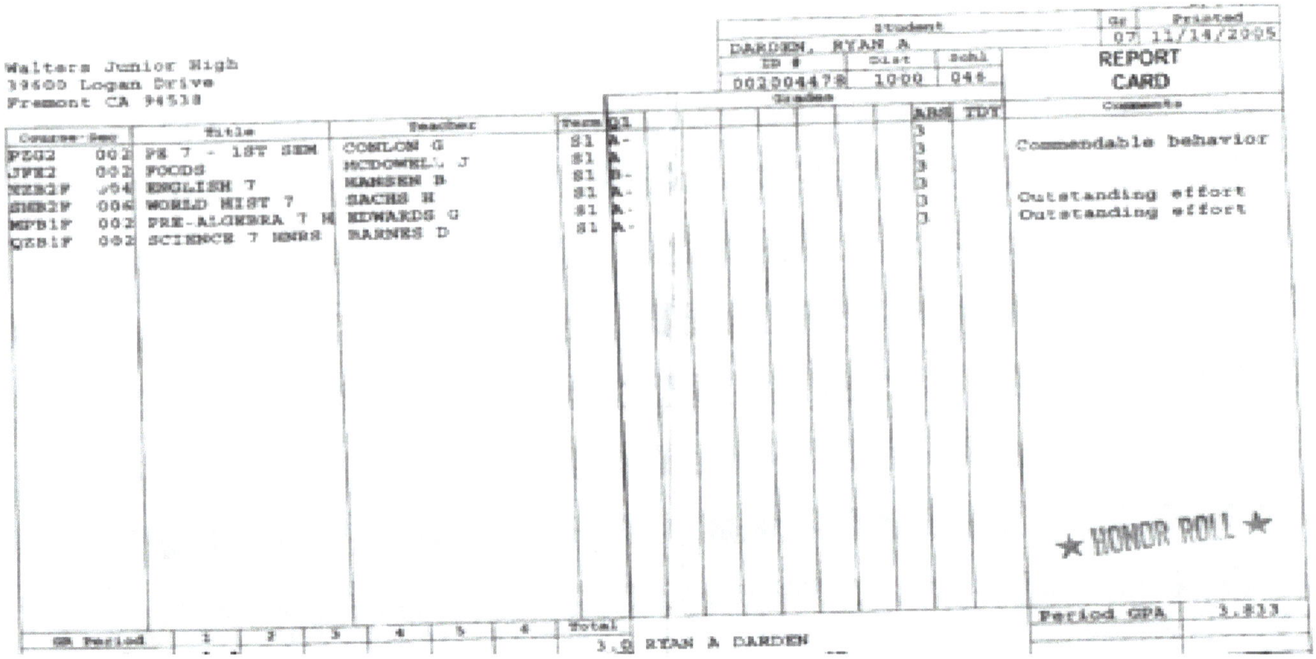

				Student			Gr	Printed
Walters Junior High				DARDEN, RYAN A			07	11/14/2005
39600 Logan Drive				ID #	Dist	Schl	REPORT CARD	
Fremont CA 94538				002004478	1000	044		
				Grades			ABS TDY	Comments
Course-Sec	Title	Teacher	Term Q1					
P2G2 002	PE 7 - 1ST SEM	CONLON G	S1 A-				3	Commendable behavior
JFE2 002	FOODS	MCDOWELL J	S1 A				3	
N2B1F 004	ENGLISH 7	HANSEN B	S1 B-				3	
S2B2F 006	WORLD HIST 7	SACHS N	S1 A-				0	Outstanding effort
MPB1F 002	PRE-ALGEBRA 7 H	EDWARDS G	S1 A				0	Outstanding effort
Q2B1F 002	SCIENCE 7 HNRS	BARNES D	S1 A-					

★ HONOR ROLL ★

Period GPA 3.833

GR Period 1 2 3 4 5 6 Total
3.0 RYAN A DARDEN

Ryan Andrew Darden

On September. 3, 2014, my son, Ryan Andrew Darden made one of the biggest decisions of his life. A decision that made me realize that he wanted to be responsible for himself and his future. Ryan decided to join the United States Army. I support my son in all he chooses to achieve and I will always be by his side. Ryan started his Basic Training the second week in September of 2014 at Fort Jackson, South Carolina (2nd Battalion 60th Infantry, Delta Co.) After only four to five weeks of training, Ryan has already shown signs of excellence. In his target shooting test, Ryan was 3rd best out of 60 soldiers. (scoring 38 out of 40). I think that's really awesome and special considering this is the first time Ryan has ever shot a firearm. Week 4 was also special. Ryan received the #1 score on his Physical Training Test out of 60 soldiers. I can see your success! My dear son, I will be there to see you graduate with honors. Ryan's next stop will be in Virginia for his training. I am so very proud of my son for taking control of his future, and I know great things are ahead for whatever he pursues.

In my early years, it was very special growing up with three beautiful and wonderful sisters. Monica, Michelle, and Marla. They are all unique in their own special way. To this day, I still cherish the great memories of our childhood. From going to church in Oakland, CA at Christ Holy Sanctified Church; to going to visit both Grandma's, Grandma Irby and Grandma Watts and my Grandfather (Gramps). Those were the days I will always remember. It wasn't until my later years that I understood why my Mom and Dad made my sisters and I attend church ALL the time. I believe they knew God would be in our hearts forever. I believe this because "it never leaves you". One of the most memorable and powerful messages I ever heard was from Pastor Stanley Long of South Bay Community Church in Fremont, CA. Briefly, his message was: "Some of us spend our whole lives trying to accomplish something to get to the top. We start climbing the ladder *"rung by rung", sometimes being frustrated wondering why we can't make it to the top; but we continue climbing and climbing and climbing. Then "finally" one day we reach our goal and make it to the top."* *ONLY TO REALIZE YOUR LADDER WAS LEANING UP AGAINST THE WRONG BUILDING.* After Pastor Long finished his sermon, the choir sang and the words remained in my spirit some 20 years later. I hope in sharing these words it will encourage and inspire my family and friends as much as it has me!

Is it all worthwhile to have food on the table and my neighbor has hunger pains
Is it all worthwhile to have fame and glory, and my living is still in vain
What does it profit a man to gain the whole world, yet turn around and lose his soul
Is it all worthwhile to say that I love you, yet I can't lend a helping hand
Is it all worthwhile to say God is my Captain, yet I can't stand my fellow man
What does it profit a man to gain the whole world, yet turn around and lose his soul

I hope these words will mean as much to you as they do to me. One thing I have come to realize is that LIVING FOR JESUS IS ALL WORTHWHILE!

My later years, has also been very special. I've had the opportunity to be reunited with my awesome brother Gabriel Christopher Darden, three more beautiful sisters Gisele Marie Darden, Diedrick Alexandra Darden, Yvette Elaine Darden Irving, and my beautiful Stepmom, Mama Ruth Darden. They are all a true blessing to have in my life. This blessing would not have been possible without the kind and giving heart of one person, my Mom (Barbara Jean Irby). Through the good times and the times of struggle, my Mom has always encouraged and taught us to have a good heart and do our best to keep in touch with our brother, sisters, and all our family. For this, I am very grateful. Thank you Mom for all your dedication and hard work in keeping together our Irby legacy.

In 1974, we moved from Oakland to San Jose, CA. My Mom always encouraged me to choose my friends wisely. Upon entering high school, I was fortunate to meet Randy Heggem. For over 40 years, I have been blessed to have the Heggem family a part of my life. My sincere thanks and appreciation to the Heggem's for welcoming me into their family.

Michelle Denise Darden-Smith
September 16, 1960, San Mateo, California
Second daughter and third child born to
Barbara Jean Irby and Samuel Darden, Jr.

I attended Elementary school in both Palo Alto, CA and BeBe Patton Christian Academy in Oakland, CA. I graduated from both Morrill Middle School and Piedmont Hills High School in San Jose, CA. I have been blessed to have one "loving" son, Durell Eugene Smith II, born January 15, 1983. I am so thankful to have a son like Durell. He is the joy of my life and all I can say is "I love you with all my heart Son". Durell's father is (Durell Eugene Smith). My son has one son, Quincy Rafael Smith, born January 20, 2007. Quincy's Mom is Loraine Smith.

I had amazing experiences with both my Grandmother and Grandfather Irby. I was about 15 years old when I wanted to go live with my Grandparents, and it was a decision that I will never regret. I felt they both needed someone to be with them, and I cherished spending time with them and wanted to love and take care of them, especially my Grandmother because she already had one of her legs amputated. No one will ever know what I went through with my Grandmother's illness, but it is something I wanted to do and I would not trade anything for those precious months being her caretaker. I was trained by nurses that came to the house and learned quickly on how to lift her in and out of her wheelchair. The loving and caring spirit I have, is what my Grandparents instilled in me, and from them, I learned more than any school books or teachers could ever have taught me.

(Continued on next page)

I still have strong memories of my Grandmother sitting looking out her living room window, waiting for me to come home from school. Church members, including the pastor of her church came often, but Grandmother would say, "oh, my helper will do that, my granddaughter will be home soon". She came to rely on me totally and only wanted me to do her special routine task. I even ironed her sheets and pillowcases, because that was one of her "forever tasks" and I took over that task with smiles. She had a special 'dust mop' that she instructed me how to dust and clean her hardwood floors. The most important part that I know for sure, is that they both taught me to show "love" and "respect" for others. Sometimes I still have a bucket of tears remembering all the sad moments just before my Grandmother passed away.

She kept saying, "someone is coming over" and she just wasn't ready to turn in for the night. I think she was expecting her children to come by, because it was Gramps birthday. She waited and waited, and then she said "I guess they are not coming". So as I was picking her up out of her wheelchair to get her ready for bed, she had a stroke right in my arms. Needless to say, I was the last person that she spoke with. I remember every moment of that evening. I remember the exact words she spoke to me, and no one will ever know how painful that experience was for me. But, for those of you that don't know, I never left her side. The ambulance came, and I rode in the ambulance with her as it hurried to the hospital. I held her hand and just wanted her to hang on and get better, because I needed her so much. I thought she would recover and be okay again, but it was not to be. When my Grandmother passed away, a part of me went with her.

Then, there was a time when my Grandfather was sick, and I was with him through some very difficult circumstances. So, I am happy that my mother (Barbara Jean Irby) chose to put this book together. It gives me great joy to be a part of it… because Grandmother and Gramps were the delight of my life and I truly miss them more than words can ever express. So to them, I say:

*"**Grandmother, I know you are resting well now, and Gramps… I will always be your 'Mitch'. Save a seat between the two of you so when I get there all will be well again. "I love you forever Grandmother and Gramps."***

(Continued on next page)

Following is an article that appeared in the Peninsula Bulletin, July 9, 1977, "A Voice of the People", regarding the care I gave my Grandmother.

Marla Colleen Wortz

February 16, 1971 - Oakland, California

Third daughter born to Barbara Jean Irby and

first daughter to Solomon Wortz, Sr.

B efore I begin, my Mom wanted to add a special note to my Dad. *I, Barbara Jean Irby, wholeheartedly thank Marla's Dad (Solomon Wortz) for his sincere commitment, honesty and Christian standards in being an extremely good Father, Friend and Provider to all four of my children. May God bless you always Solomon, Jeanette and your children. (Jeanette, I thank you too for being a "special other Mom" to Marla, Samuel, Michelle and Monica. You are loved dearly by all of us and thanks too for your sincere friendship to me.*

What a blessed life I have had thus far. I have one awesome son, Marchel Jonery Robinson, born November 25, 1995, born to Marla Colleen Wortz and Mike Robinson. I graduated from Piedmont Hills High school in San Jose, CA.

Me with my Dad and Mom

On July 12, 2003, I graduated from University of Phoenix (Sacramento Valley Campus) receiving my Bachelor of Science Degree in Business Accounting. I was extremely proud that both my parents were present at the graduation ceremony, including my siblings and Godmother along with other relatives and close friends.

Piedmont Hills High School
Graduation, 1989

Childhood and Teenage Activities: Sports: Soccer, Softball, and Basketball
(Samuel thank you for taking your baby sister along with you when going to play your sports.)

Music: Clarinet and Piano
Education
College:
- Morris Brown College, Atlanta, Georgia
- University of Phoenix, Sacramento, California *(Degree: Bachelor of Science in Accounting)*

Accomplishments:
- Basketball Team Mother for Durell and Marchel: San Jose, California and Stockton, California
- Former Sole Proprietor (Pre-employment training for Youth and Business Consultant) Stockton, California
- Volunteer Instructor at a Women's Shelter: Stockton, California
- Volunteer for various events within the Stockton Community

Marital Status:
Divorced (married to Shawn Curry on May 16, 2009)

(Continued on next page)

Me and my Mom

Me with my Godmother Vivian

Thank you mom for being the amazing, wonderful, and God fearing woman that has raised her children to be respectful, caring, and loving. No matter of the life situations your children have or will experience you taught us to always be there for one another. You've instilled in us to say, "I love You" before getting off the phone or leaving from our family visit. I'm so very proud and honored to have you as my Mother. You did an awesome job in raising me for the woman I am today. Your enormous heart and love to help others made an impact on my life choices and enabled me to raise a respectful and loving son. I'm so proud to be the Mother of my son, Marchel J. Robinson. I love you son with all my heart and thank you for always being respectful, obedient, and well mannered. Our relationship as a mother and son is GREAT! Continue to put your trust in the Lord. I am now a grandmother and I know Marchel will be a great father. He will teach his child the same loving qualities he learned from me that was instilled through my Mom and Dad. I love you Ava!

Although, I was forced to be in church from birth to 17, I'm thankful to Mom and Dad for keeping me in the Word. A Mother's prayer never ends. We've developed a prayer partnership over the years and glad that without judgment we can pray for those in need of a blessing. Without much thought, I've taken on the same attributes from my mother, such as working with children in the church and working with the women in the shelter.

To my siblings: Monica, Samuel, & Michelle thank you for your continuous love and support. I love you all very much and you can always count on me. My nephews: Richard, Durell, Andre, and Ryan I love you very much and will always be there for you. I'm so proud to be a Great Auntie to Quincy Rafael Smith and Richelle Barbara Myers. I love you both and will be there for you as I have with your fathers.

(Continued on next page)

Mommy, Mom, Mother Dear, please always know that I love you with all my heart and you will always be taken care of through long or short distance. Daddy, your strong faith as a Christian man goes unspoken. No matter of the circumstances in my life you have always without fail prayed for me over the phone or in person. Thank you, Daddy for your love, support and especially being an active father in my life. I've learned from both of my parents to stay positive, do not worry, and give it to the Lord.

I know my comments are lengthy, but if you didn't know; now you know that FAMILY means so very much to me. I can't stop without saying thank you to Gramps and Grandmother for being so loving and caring. I LOVE YOU! In 1981, my Mom took on the role as Soccer Coach for my San Jose North Valley Soccer Team (Dynamites). What an amazing Mom I have!

Finally, Mom, thank you for taking on this wonderful project and giving us the opportunity to learn more about our family history. I'm so Blessed and honored to be a part of the Irby-Looney Family. WE ARE FAMILY!

Marchel Jonery Robinson
November 25, 1995 - Santa Clara, CA

Education:
Campbell Elementary School: Campbell, CA
San Joaquin Elementary School: Stockton, CA - Graduated May 29, 2009
Kimball High School: Tracy, CA while attending my elementary school I took up an interest in playing chess and joined the chess club. My Uncle Sam taught me how to play chess. My mother got me into sports at an early age. I played the following sports: Flag Football, T-Ball, Basketball (private league and church league)

I graduated from Kimball High School in Tracy, California on June 2, 2013. After graduating from high school, I attended Santa Monica College for a year. I completed my first year of college with a 3.35 GPA. I returned home to work and provide for my daughter born on April 24, 2015. I'm continuing my education by taking online courses at Santa Monica College. It is my plan to receive my AA transfer and attend a four year college. I'm not sure where, but it will be somewhere in Northern or Southern CA.

Racially Profiled
While attending Santa Monica College, I lived in the dorms near UCLA. My God-mother told me and my best friend to be very careful when walking in the Westwood area. She said the police are racist and to watch ourselves. A week later a couple of my friends were walking around the Westwood area. We were walking with a white female and my two other friends are Black. We were stopped by the police and questioned. The Police Officers said they stopped us because one of my friends was walking with an opened beer can. The Police Officer told him the can has to be in a paper bag. My friend was from Atlanta, Georgia and said he was not aware of the law in California. We had to show our ID's while our white female friend was asked to stand to the side. The Police Officer let my other friend and I go, while they continued talking to my friend from Atlanta. The Officers eventually let him go, but we all knew that we were racially profiled because we were three black men walking with a white female. That was my first time being racially profiled and was shaken up by the experience. Before that horrible experience my Mom told me that if I'm ever stopped by the police to be respectful and answer the questions truthfully.

(Continued on next page)

The struggle continues with our Black men, and I hope one day we as Black men can walk and drive down the street without being profiled or killed for senseless reasons.

At a young age my mother took me to her former business where she trained teenagers on pre-employment and presentation skills. I also had the opportunity to see her work with the women at the shelter. My mother had me speak in front of the church for various programs such as Black History Month and the Sunday School/Youth Annual Day. I was asked to give a presentation for the Men's Annual Day at church, as I had the opportunity in 2012 to attend the 100 Black Men Young Male Black Conference in Sacramento, California. The personal training and speaking events allowed me to excel when preparing for reports and presentations in high school, college, and church. With receiving positive feedback from church members and peers; I decided to major in Communications during my second semester at Santa Monica College. In high school, I developed an interest in drawing and playing the keyboard. This remains a hobby of mine and I may pursue as a side business.

Marchel, Monique and our baby Ava

(Continued on next page)

As I'm writing my history, within 60 days I will become a father. I'm 19, and the mother of my child (Monique Creantor) and I have taken the responsibility to work and make sure that our daughter will not only be financially cared for, but have our unconditional love and support. I know it's going to be hard, but my Mom told me this is a minor setback and it's up to me to stay motivated and see my goals through.

I'm glad my Mom brought me up in church as my Christian faith has helped me through some difficult challenges. I know God will not leave me while I learn how to be a good role model to my daughter. Ava Marielle Robinson was born on April 24, 2015 at San Joaquin Hospital in French Camp, California.

I would like to share with my family members, relatives, and friends or anyone that is a fatherless or motherless child to not give up in life. Find a trustworthy relative or friend to support you and help you through the challenging experiences. My Dad was not active in my life and missed out on a lot of sport games, award recognition at school, and sharing the day to day moments. My Mother always allowed me to express how I felt and always gave me the option to see my Dad when I wanted to. I'm thankful for having a loving Mother that made sure I was cared for, and she was there for me every step of the way. It is my goal to become a motivational speaker to help people overcome obstacles and succeed in life.

Thank you Grandma for making this possible! I love you! *A bushel and a peck and a hug around the neck — Grandma and Grandson moments*

Memories

Memories

Memories

Mother & Dad on a train trip

Daddy, Joanne and myself at Nichol Park in Richmond, California. Daddy saw to it that we were exposed to everything there was to offer, such as Parks, Ice Follies, Zoo, Ringling Brothers Barnum & Bailey Circus and many other educational events.

Me and my sister, Joanne

These are the steps that took us up to our 1940's home. "The Projects" 700 South 24th Street, Richmond, CA

1950-1960's Mother trying out her 'luck' in Reno, Nevada

Memories

Memories

After Mother passed away, Daddy sold our family home and moved into this high-rise apartment building in Oakland, California. If you look real close, you could see Daddy waving to me as I took this picture. (from right side, third row over and third balcony up).

Memories

Daddy built this little house in our back yard at 1036 Laurel Avenue, Palo Alto, California and this is where he kept all his gardening tools, lawn furniture and other miscellaneous items. In 2012, I made a trip to California and knocked on the door at "1036 Laurel Avenue" and spoke with the current resident, she was very generous and allowed me to walk through the house and out the side door to the backyard. Monica was with me, and I was so excited to see that the house still stands in the backyard just as Daddy built it. It was a blessing to be allowed to take pictures of *"Daddy's House"*. You can see that Daddy was indeed a fine carpenter.

Touch somebody's life with goodness and kindness --you will never regret it! I am blessed daily with beautiful memories of special friends God placed in my life. My life journey would not have been complete without them.

First, there are no words to describe the love and admiration I have for Glenn Cole. He has been there for me for the past 39 years and we have an amazing friendship. I took on the roll as his "Other Mom" when he came to Stanford as a student, and that is the way it remains to this day (2015). Glenn married Holly Delaney after he graduated from Stanford University and they have two awesome sons, Jeremy and Evan Cole. Thanks Glenn and Holly for loving and caring about me all these years.

A message from my Adopted Son (Glenn Phillip Cole) March 6, 2012

"We first met my freshman year at Stanford in 1975. My freshman advisor was Mike McHargue who you worked for at the Learning Assistance Center. I took a work study job at the LAC and you were my boss. I think Marla may have been 4 or 6 years old then and she was as cute as a button and still is. You and I remained friends throughout my whole time at Stanford and I subsequently met all of your children and other members of your family. You met a few members of my family also at my graduation in 1979, including my mother and my older sister. My mother was pleased that I had found such a nice person while I was away at school. I could always count on you to be a friend and to treat me like family. You did that for many of the Black students at Stanford but I really appreciated it since I was so far from home. I will always remember your kindness and willingness to help others while asking for nothing in return. Love, Glenn."

Others that have touched my life deeply and remain dear to my heart are:

- Vivian Dansby-McCathrion - My oldest female friend from 1940's Project Housing
- Carl Wright - My oldest male friend from the 1940's Project Housing
- Prof. Oscar Buneman (deceased) - 1960's Greatest Boss and friend from Stanford University
- Ray Newbill - My adopted brother since 1950's.
- Jacquelyn Tate - High School friend since 1950's. She set a family tradition by singing *"His Eye is on the Sparrow"* for the Homegoing Celebration for my mother, father, brother Robert as well as for my nephew Norris Irby. Thank you JT.
- Keith Sparks - Stanford student and adopted son
- Ricky & Donna Harris - My other adopted children
- Lamonte & Phyllis Wiley - Co-worker and adopted family
- Christia Carroll - "Avon Calling" friend
- Herb Ruffin - Always a devoted friend
- Helen Eldridge - Devoted friend
- Juanita Bond - Church friend and adopted Sis
- Prof. Horace Porter & Carla - Stanford University, superb boss and dear friends forever
- Mr. & Mrs. Vern Jordan - God's Amazing Chosen Landlord since December 1, 2013
- Chris and Jennifer Simon - Absolute God sent friends
- William Watts - Brother-in-law
- Gary and Robbyn Banks - My adopted son and daughter from South Bay Church, Fremont, CA
- Cheryl French - Amazing Sister and friend
- Williams Family (George, Gloria, Debbie, and Wally) - Friends forever
- Marsha B. Bell - Praises, through thick and thin, we remain sisters and friends still

My list goes on and on, and just by chance, you are reading this and don't see your name, don't worry, because you are tucked away in my heart forever and I will never ever forget you.

Pictured are my long-time friends, the Dansby sisters and their father. I met them back in early 1940's. Vivian (far right) is an unbelievable friend and extremely kind to my children and Godmother to my daughter Marla, and known as "Aunt Vivian" by all my children. Thanks be to God for a lasting friendship for over 70 plus years, and nothing has damaged our friendship or the respect we have for each other.

After all is said and done, I am tremendously grateful and thank God for my four children. The Lord trusted me to raise, love and nourish them, and I have given them my best! So to Monica, Samuel, Michelle and Marla, all four of you are the best gifts I have received. Each of you are so very different, and the most important part is, you are mine! I love you and very proud to be your Mother. Never forget the love I freely share and have shared with you because love never fails, and my heart is filled with praise daily because of you, my children, grand-children, great-grand children. To my five grandsons and one great-grandson, you each light up my life and I am proud to be called "Mom, Mommy, Grandma and Granny." Last but not least, I am so honored to have three beautiful great-granddaughters. Hold tight to each other and keep our family together always with love and admiration. Finally, my soul was made content when I found the Lord and one of these old days, I pray the Lord will say "well done my good and faithful Barbara. I pray that the work I have done will speak for me.

All my love,
Mom
Barbara Jean Irby

I trust in you, Oh Lord. You are my God. My time is in your hands.
Psalms 31: 14-15

Joanne Marie Irby-Ikner

June 12, 1940 - Springfield, Missouri

Fourth daughter and eighth child born to Ulysses Grant and Edna Looney Irby

I am the youngest of eight children born to the union of Ulysses Grant and Edna Looney Irby. The family moved to Richmond, California when I was two years old. At the age of nine, I accepted Jesus into my heart. Our family were members of the A.M.E. Church in Richmond. I attended Nystrom Elementary School and Roosevelt Junior High School in Richmond. In 1955 we moved to East Palo Alto, California. Our family joined the A.M.E. Zion Methodist Church in Palo Alto proper, and we had a wonderful pastor by the name of Rev. J. Oliver Hart. I was a Junior in high school when we relocated and I attended Menlo-Atherton High School in Atherton, California.

After graduating from Menlo Atherton in 1958, I attended Foothill Junior College in Mountain View, CA. I was subsequently employed at Varian Associates in Palo Alto. In 1960, I went to work for Lockheed Missiles and Space in Sunnyvale, CA and worked there for eight years.

On April 8, 1962, I married my husband, John L. Ikner, and April 8, 2015 we celebrated 53 years of marriage. Two daughters were born to this union. Nicole Marie Ikner, born on November 7, 1968 and Nolana Marie Ikner, born on July 18, 1971.

(Continued on next page)

IRBY'S DELUXE CHILI
Ulysses G. Irby
Oakland, CA

Ingredients
- 4 pounds pinto beans
- 10 cups canned tomatoes
- 2 pounds chopped green peppers
- 4 tablespoons salad oil
- 4 pounds chopped onions
- 4 cloves crushed garlic
- 1-1/2 cups chopped parsley
- 1/2 pound butter
- 5 pounds coarse ground chuck beef (or chili grind)
- 2 pounds coarse ground lean pork
- 1 cup chili powder
- 4 tablespoons salt
- 3 teaspoons pepper
- 3 teaspoons cumin seed
- 3 teaspoons accent

My Mother was a wonderful person who loved all her children so much. She always enjoyed hearing stories about us and later about her grandchildren. She was a wonderful cook and we enjoyed many great meals with her and Daddy on Sunday afternoons. Daddy was also a great cook and a loving Father. His specialties were "chicken pot pies" and homemade chili. Daddy submitted his chili recipe for a Church Cookbook in 1983, which was created by my sister, Barbara. Along with her, we proudly share his Chili recipe with each of you. It was always the best chili and we hope you will try making it… "you'll be glad you did." Daddy also enjoyed making and serving his delicious 'eggnog' for company as they entered the house.

Dad serving his famous eggnog

IRBY'S DELUX CHILI (CONTINUED)

Preparation

Wash beans, soak overnight in water simmer covered in same water until tender. Add tomatoes and simmer ten minutes. Saute' green pepper in salad oil five minutes. Add onions cook until tender, stirring often. Add garlic and parsley

Melt butter and saute' meat for twenty minutes. Add meat to onion mixture, stir in chili powder and cook for ten minutes. Add this to beans and add spices. Simmer covered for one hour. Cook uncovered for one-half hour. Skim excess fat from top and serve. Better second day.
Yields: 40 to 50 bowls

COOKED, EATEN AND ENJOYED FOR 28 YEARS!

 Daddy was a master carpenter and welder. He made steel lunch boxes for me and my sister, Barbara. We both carried our lunch in it to school.

I have great memories of my Grandmother Looney also. She was really special, and I remember spending the summer with her one year before I was of school age. My birthday came while I was there, and since no children lived nearby, she and my aunts (Zelia, Matteal and Tillie) dressed in frilly dresses and had a party for me. We had a lot of fun and played games on the lawn. I also remember how she would lay me on her kitchen table with my head extended over the edge, and she would wash my hair. Then we would go out on the porch where she would braid and dry it.

While home raising our daughters, I enrolled in a Home Study course for Interior Decorating with La Salle University and received my Diploma of Completion. I did freelance work for a while and later went to work for JC Penney Store as an Interior Decorator where I worked for 5 years. When I left JC Penney, I went to work for Ravenswood City School District in Palo Alto, California as a Confidential Secretary. I also worked for the San Jose School District in 1996 as an Administrative Assistant.

As an adult, I joined First A.M.E. Methodist Church in San Jose, California and while there, I received my ordination as Deaconess and served on the Communion Ministry. In December of 1996, I moved my membership to South Bay Community Church in Fremont, California and serve on the Communion Ministry. For the past eight years, I have served as Servant Leader and remain an active and dedicated member. I am also a member of 'ASAM' --(Adult Senior Active Ministry) at South Bay and I belong to a small group as well.

(Continued on next page)

My hobbies are reading, traveling and playing scrabble. I am a lover of words, and there are times when a few of my friends and myself will play scrabble way into the "wee hours of the morning". I also enjoy bowling, movies, plays and eating out with family and friends. My siblings are pictured below:

Barbara, Robert, me and Joe

Robert, Junior, Joe and me

Now, I share my two daughters, Nicole and Nolana, along with my precious granddaughters, Avery and Sydney. Hope you enjoy!

Nicole Marie Ikner
November 7, 1968 - Palo Alto, California
Daughter to John L. and Joanne M. Ikner

I was born at Stanford Hospital in Palo Alto, California to John and Joanne Ikner. I grew up in Sunnyvale, California, and graduated from Cupertino High School, in Cupertino, California. I accepted Christ as my personal savior during college and have been walking with Him ever since.

I attended De Anza College and graduated with an AA degree. After graduating from De Anza, I transferred to Howard University in Washington, DC and graduated in 1993 with a BFA degree.

Howard University Graduation Washington, DC

I have been employed with Intuit, Inc., in Mountain View, CA since July 1998 and am currently working as an Executive Assistant for the Vice President of Intuit Labs.

On September 6, 2002, Aaron Ware and I were married.

Bride and Groom —Nicole and Aaron

Ed and Sandra Ware, pictured below are the parents of my husband Aaron. They just celebrated their wedding anniversary on December 10, 2014. They live in Oakland, California and attend New Beginnings Community Church. They have two children, Aaron and Tatiana Ware.

I have traveled to Mexico, Japan, Spain, London and have an upcoming trip to South Africa in October 2014. Aaron and I enjoyed a fabulous trip to Japan together.

Nolana Marie Ikner-Newell
July 18, 1971 - Carmel, California
Daughter to John L. and Joanne M. Ikner

I am so blessed to have two phenomenal parents, Joanne and John Ikner, who both have raised me to be the woman I am today. I salute them for being loving and caring parents. Not only have they been the perfect parents to me and my sister, Nicole, they are also the ideal Grandmother and Grandfather for my two daughters. Thanks a million, Mom and Dad.

Delie Green (John's Grandmother) and Paternal Great-Grandmother to Nolana and Nicole. Delie passed away at age 102.

Four Ikner Generations

Lula D. Ikner (John's mother), John L. Ikner, Sydney Maxine Newell and Nolana. Lula passed away at age 96. We all were richly blessed to have known Lula D. Ikner. May her soul always rest in perfect peace with the Lord. *(If there are pecan trees in Heaven… then Lula will be picking and saving some for us when we join her).*

I graduated from Cupertino High School and then Howard University.

Howard University Graduation

After graduating from Howard University, I went on to get my MA/Ed degree from George Mason University in the year 2000. George Mason University is the largest research university in Virginia and is based in unincorporated Fairfax County, Virginia. The university's motto is Freedom and Learning. The University was founded as a branch of the University of Virginia in 1957 and became an independent institution in 1972. Today Mason is recognized for its strong programs in economics, law, creative writing, computer science and business.

Maxine (deceased) and Ralph Leon Newell Sr.
Precious Memories of Maxine will always be with us…
Wonderful, Remarkable and Worthy Mom, Wife, Grandmother and Friend

On July 20, 1996, I married Ralph Leon Newell, Jr. We are the proud parents of two daughters, who are exceptionally good children and students. Sydney Maxine Newell, born January 3, 2002 and Avery Marie Newell born July 14, 2004. Pictured are Ralph's parents, our children's Grandparents. Maxine (deceased) and Ralph Leon Newell Sr. Precious Memories of Maxine will always be with us.

Ralph and Nolana enjoying each other

And now, there is no greater joy for Ralph and I than to present our two wonderful daughters to you. We are proud of them and thank God daily for giving us the opportunity to raise, nourish and provide a safe and loving home for them.

My name is **Sydney Newell**, daughter of Ralph and Nolana Newell, and I turned 13 years old on January 3, 2015. I'm in 7th grade. I live in Virginia and my parents are Ralph and Nolana Newell. I attend Christ Chapel Academy and I'm a straight A student. I am in NJHS, which stands for National Junior Honor Society. It is an organization for students with great grades, and who are leaders with their peers. It is an organization in which we serve others. We have food drives and other things to help the less fortunate. We also volunteer for stuff around school. I am also a cadet in Girl Scouts so give me a call during cookie season in the Spring! I also am a Semi-Black belt in Tae Kwon Doe and I play the B-flat clarinet. I love to visit the Smithsonian Museums in D.C. When I grow up I want to be a chemist, biochemist, or bacteriologist. I wish to attend Thomas Jefferson High School. It is a school for advanced science, math and technology and it is the best school in the state and 4th best in the country. For college I want to attend Yale, Princeton, or Harvard. Some places I've been include; Mexico, Canada, about half the states in the United States including Alaska, and going on Disney cruises.

I'm **Avery Newell**. I'm 10 years old and my birthday is July 14. I am in 5th grade at Christ Chapel Academy. I like computers, books, and crafts. I like to ride my bike outside and draw. I made the A and B honor roll. I take Tae Kwon Do and I'm a semi-Black belt. I'm a junior in Girl Scouts with a really fun troop. I love to visit the American Girl store. When I grow up I want to be a dentist or veterinarian. I would like to go to Yale. Last summer I visited the Grand Canyon and stepped on the four Corners of Arizona, Colorado, New Mexico, and Utah.

MEMORIES

Sydney and Avery, Grand Canyon, Summer 2013

Sydney and Avery sharing their awesome father Ralph Newell

MEMORIES

Bahamas

Japan

Hawaii

Egypt

MEMORIES

In October 2012, I traveled to the Holy Land where we cruised to Egypt, Italy, Israel, Turkey and Greece. While we were in Egypt, I had the great joy of being baptized in the Jordan River (the fish that were in the River were nibbling at my feet). It was truly a trip of a life time. Our trips, adventures and journey's go on and on, and Nicole and I want to share our trip to South Africa in October 2014. It was an amazing adventure. We have heard it said that when you are there, you leave a piece of your heart. We both agree with that statement. The country is so beautiful and vast. We went on two safari trips and they were truly awesome. The big treat was to see the male lion as he rose from his nap and walked through the tall grass out into the open and lay down again. Cameras were flashing in our jeep as we looked on fascinated. We wound around the corner and discovered two female lionesses lying right in front of us. They were close enough to touch. They stayed where they were as pictures were taken of them, "thank goodness." There were so many memorable experiences, but two that stood out were the visits to Nelson Mandela's home and to the Apartheid Museum. One of the excerpts on the wall stated that "The most potent weapon in the hands of the oppressor is the mind of the oppressed". It was very emotional to walk around and see and read what our people went through. The museum portrayed in vivid detail the triumph of the human spirit over adversity.

MEMORIES

MEMORIES

Lord, I thank you for blessing me to make this marvelous trip to South Africa!

MEMORIES

MEMORIES

Women demonstrating how they carry water on their heads

Nicole with Sheila—having their first experience 'behind bars' in Robben Island Jail

MEMORIES

Shakaland, Zulu Tribe – (believe in Polygamy)

Taking a break under the Elephant Tusk

It is my prayer that you will go with confidence in the direction of your dreams. With God as your guide, live the life He has planned for you. I thank God for my husband, John and my daughters and granddaughters. We hope you have been enriched to the fullest with sharing our adventures and lives with you!

God Bless You,

Joanne Marie Irby-Ikner

"We are the Irby Family"

We are blessed to have each other;
No one in this book
will ever be replaced by
Someone else
You each are unique individuals
With great value and importance
Created in the image God intended
Through thick and thin
Come hell or high water
For now and even after the end
We must always stand tall —and remain together

We are the Irby's

Barbara Jean Irby

December 2015

Celebrating the Life
of
Ulysses Irby

When the trumpet of the Lord shall sound, and time shall be no more,
When the saved of Earth shall gather over on the other shore,
and the roll is called up yonder, I'll be there...

"Junior"

Alpha	Omega
August 30, 1924	April 29, 2015

Services Held
Friday -- May 8, 2015 -- 11:00 AM
at

Jerusalem Baptist Church
398 Sheridan Avenue
Palo Alto, CA 94306

Reverend Emil Thomas, Officiating

Obituary

Ulysses Irby was born on August 30, 1924 in Springfield, Missouri to Ulysses Grant and Edna Looney Irby. He passed away peacefully at home in the presence of his faithful wife who was by his side continuously until the end. Both his mother and father, two sisters (Colleen and Opal) and two brothers (Charles Henry and Robert Lee) all preceded him in death.

Ulysses attended Lincoln School in Springfield, Missouri. He moved with his parents and siblings to Richmond, CA in 1942. On April 1, 1949 he married Christia B. Rose and they are the parents of five children. Ulysses united with and was baptized at Victory Missionary Baptist Church in Las Vegas, NV on November 28, 2004. Being a born-again Christian was unspeakable joy to him. Ulysses first worked at Kaiser Shipyards in Richmond, CA and later worked for the United States Postal Service in Palo Alto for several years. He retired from Great Western Financial Corporation where he worked from 1976 to 1989 as an Appraiser. He was a hard and dedicated worker all of his life starting at about the age of seventeen. Ulysses lived his life to the fullest, travelling to various places, camping at Thousand Trails, and attending yearly Family Reunions in Oklahoma City. Family gatherings with food and good times was important to him, and his son Norris would say… "pops can cook". Ulysses was so full of 'humor' and he could really pull a fast one on you if you hung around him long enough! When it came to sports, he played baseball, and was a great bowler with many trophies. He had great admiration for the San Francisco Giants and San Francisco 49er's. He loved music and especially Gospel and Jazz. Remembering family birthdays and anniversaries was important to him and he took great pride in making sure his family and siblings received cards every year. During his last days, Ulysses was surrounded by his family members and friends.

He leaves to cherish his memory, his wife Christia of 66 years, one daughter, Shirley Irby-Tomlin (Huling Tomlin/deceased), four sons, Adrian Norris Irby, Sr. (Diane Marie Bundy-Irby /deceased) Richard Maurice Irby (Cynthia Irby/deceased), Andre Danneal Irby (Kathy Martinez) and Lawrence Christopher Irby, Sr. (Cherise Irby); two sisters, Joanne Irby-Ikner (John Ikner), Barbara Jean Irby and one brother, Joe Bill Irby (Betty J. Irby); three grandsons, Anthony Lorenzo Robertson, Adrian Norris Irby Jr. (British Nicole Irby) Lawrence Christopher Irby, Jr; seven granddaughters, Christia Naomi Robertson, Brooke Rose Irby-Tomlin, Tanisha Lorraine Irby-Worthy (Jermain Milton Worthy), Kiana Leilani Irby, Adriana Lynn Irby, Lauren Christia Irby and Jazmine Ferguson; seventeen great-grandchildren and a *multitude* of nieces, nephews, cousins and friends.

TO GOD BE THE GLORY

Pallbearers

Alex Carter -- Michael Irby -- Byron Roberts
Chris Siguer -- Lawrence Stanton -- Jermaine Worthy

Honorary Pallbearers

Adrian Norris Irby, Sr -- Richard Maurice Irby -- Andre Danneal Irby
Lawrence Christopher Irby, Sr., -- Anthony Lorenzo Robertson
Adrian Norris Irby, Jr. -- Samuel Darden III -- Darrell Glenn Irby
Eric Russell Irby -- Roman L. Irby-Heagler -- Dwayne Everett Irby
John L. Ikner -- George Brown -- Fred Johnson

Acknowledgment

The family of Ulysses Irby wishes to express with grateful hearts our sincere appreciation and thanks for the many acts of kindness and expressions of sympathy extended during this time of bereavement.

Interment

Skylawn Memorial Park
Highway 92 at Skyline Blvd.
San Mateo, CA 94402

Services Under the Direction of

Jones Mortuary
660 Donohoe Street
E. Palo Alto, CA 94303

Order of Service

Quiet Music

Processional

Hymn of Comfort.. *Blessed Assurance*

Scriptures:
> Old Testament 23 Psalms
> New Testament John 14: 1-3

Prayer of Comfort...Minister

Congregational Hymn..."Hold to God's Unchanging Hand"

Special Expressions.."As a Dad"
> Lawrence Christopher Irby, Sr. and Richard Maurice Irby

...."As a Brother"
> Barbara Jean Irby

Musical Selection..."In Times Like These"

Resolutions and Acknowledgements

Obituary...Read Silently

Solo...Clara Rice
> *His Eye is on the Sparrow*

Eulogy...Pastor Emil Thomas

Invitation to Discipleship

Recessional.."When We All Get to Heaven"

Cry Not *(Author Unknown)*

Cry not for though you love me my Saviour loves me more.
I've journeyed far to be with Him, now I'm approaching Heaven's door.
He saw fit to prepare a place for me where there's no sorrow, pain or strife.
So, I leave you not to mourn a death but to rejoice for my brand new life.
Look down upon my mortal remains and ask not the questions why.
For it was the shell that held my earthly form, my soul it did not die.
Grieve not for this old body, it will return from whence it came.
But my spirit will soar in the Heavens and I'll rejoice in my Saviour's name.

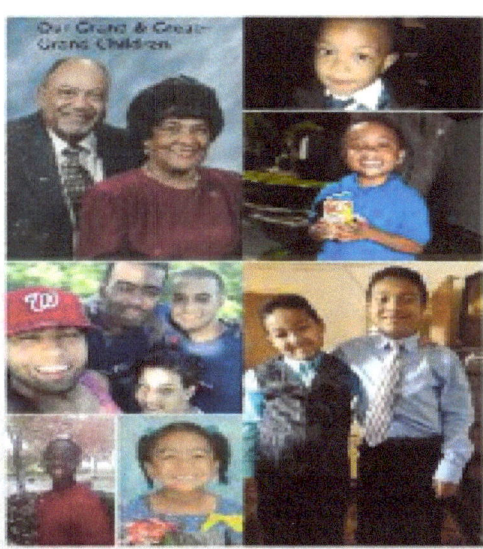

The Irby Family

About the author..

Barbara Jean Irby

Barbara Jean Irby took her time to compile this tremendous account of her wonderful family. Her insights and tremendous love for her family could not be contained and pours out in this book, *Our Irby Legacy*. Barbara makes the investment of documenting the Irby family heritage in this book as told from each of her siblings. Smart, loving, intelligent, and committed are words that summarize the way family members and friends feel about Barbara. She is deeply appreciative to each of her family members for sharing their powerful story. Barbara currently retired and lives in North Las Vegas, Nevada.

INDEX

A
Adams, Billy Jr., 31
Allen, Andre Marel, 121, 125, 147

B
Barber, Derrick Andre, 102
Bedell-Looney, Lillie Mae, 23, 122
Bedell, Mary Cavin, 22
Bundy, Diane Marie, 58, 60

C
Carter, Tommy, 81
Cole, Glenn Phillip, 150
Creantor, Monique, 142

D
Darden, Ryan Andrew, 121, 128, 131
Darden Samuell III 121, 122, 138, 129
Darden-Batchelor, Monica Ann, 121, 122, 123, 126, 145, 147
Darden-Smith, Michelle Denise 76, 121, 133, 134, 136, 144, 145
Durand, Carol Joan 152

F
Ferguson-Irby, Jazmine, 71, 72

G
Gaines, Dorthy E., 152
Green, Delle, 164

H
Hall, Craig Jr. 82, 86
Hall, Craig Sr., 86
Willis-Hall, Lisa, 82, 86
Heagler-Irby, Romond L. Sr., 80
Heagler-Stevens, Valerie, 80

I
Ikner, John L., 32, 155, 160, 164, 165, 169, 170, 172
Ikner, Lula D., 164
Ikner,-Newell, Nolana Marie, 163, 164, 165, 166, 167, 170, 172

Irby, Adrian Norris, Jr. 59, 64, 65
Irby, Adrian Norris, Sr., 48, 58, 61, 72
Irby, Adrian Rashaad (AR), 65
Irby, Adriana Lynn 68, 69
Irby, Andre Danneal, 48, 68, 73
Irby, Andrea Denise 98, 102, 106, 108
Irby, Barbara Jean, 29, 30, 32, 35, 68, 72, 87, 106, 107, 111, 112, 116, 121, 127, 136, 137, 139, 140, 145, 146, 147, 149, 152, 157, 172, 185
Irby, Betty J., 97, 104
Irby, Charles Henry, 27
Irby, Cherise 70, 72
Irby, Christia B. 45, 47, 68, 72
Irby, Colleen May, 29
Irby Daezella Patrice 86
Irby, Darrell Glen, 98, 99, 106
Irby, Davonni, 84
Irby, Dwayne Everett, 84, 85, 86, 888
Irby, Edna Looney, 21, 25, 30, 32, 35, 36, 38, 44, 72, 73, 96, 106, 134, 145, 146
Irby, Eric Russell, 98, 100, 107, 108
Irby, Erica Rose, 101
Irby, Blanche, 31
Irby, Grace, 27, 31
Irby, Henry Garrett 5, 12, 13
Irby, Janiece, 84
Irby, Joe B., 30, 32, 91, 95, 96, 97, 104, 107, 158
Irby, Jamie, 85, 86
Irby, Julian Garrett, 21, 31, 35, 87, 106
Irby, Kathryn, 31
Irby, Kiana Leilani, 68, 69
Irby, Lauren Christia, 71, 73
Irby, Lawrence Christopher, Jr., 32, 71, 72, 73
Irby, Lawrence Christopher, Sr., 68, 70, 73
Irby, Mamie, 31
Irby, Mary Gipson, 5, 17
Irby, Michael Anthony, 83, 88
Irby, Mikiya, 83
Irby, Opal, 29
Irby, Priscilla, 100
Irby, Priscilla Elizabeth, 101
Irby, Richard Maurice, 48, 66, 72
Irby, Robert Lee, 29, 32, 72, 73, 75, 76, 78, 86, 87, 89, 105, 144, 158
Irby, Shayla, 85, 86
Irby-Worth, Tanisha Lorraine, 59, 63, 72, 73
Irby, Ulysses (JR), 39, 41, 42, 44, 45, 47, 52, 68, 72, 73, 78, 86, 95, 107, 158, 179

INDEX

Irby, Ulysses Grant, 12, 14, 19, 21, 30, 31, 32, 35, 36, 37, 38, 44, 73, 87, 92, 95, 105, 106, 112, 144, 147, 148, 156, 157, 172
Irby, Vernon Garrett, 35, 106
Irby, Veronica Catherine, 101
Irby, Zoey Asana, 65
Irby-Alex, Druella 77, 78, 87, 88
Irby-Bundy, Diane Marie, 60, 61
Irby-Carter, Lorraine Marie, 81, 88
Irby-Clark, Rose Mary, 10
Irby-Hall, Tonya Carol, 82, 86
Irby-Ikner, Joanne Marie, 29, 30, 32, 35, 72, 87, 107, 146, 152, 155, 157, 158, 160, 165, 167, 169, 170, 171, 172, 173, 174, 176
Irby-Robbins, Charlotte Veronica, 98, 99, 105, 106, 107, 108
Irby-Tomlin, Shirley Ann 48, 49, 68, 72, 73
Irby-Williams, British 64, 65

J
Jackson, Ella 103
James, Devanar, 81

K
King, Mason Aaron, 52, 57, 73

L
Looney, Charles Benjamin, Sr., 24
Looney, Matteal, 32, 172
Looney, Roy T., 92, 172
Looney, Tillie, 32, 172
Looney-Adams, Mary Sue, 11

M
Martinez, Kathy, 69
McCathrion, Vivian Y., 139, 152
Mitchell, Rufus, 31, 73, 106
Myers, Richard Doron, Jr., 121, 124, 126, 144, 147
Myers, Richelle Barbara, 121, 126

N
Newell, Avery 168, 169, 172
Newell, Maxine, 166
Newell, Ralph Leon, Jr., 166, 167, 169
Newell, Ralph Leon, Sr., 166
Newell, Sydner Maxine, 164, 168, 169, 170, 172

P
Pitts, Shaun, 82

R
Robertson, Anthony, 50
Robertson, Anthony Lorenzo, 50
Robertson, Christian, 50
Robertson, Cheyenne, 50
Robertson, Christia Naomi, 51, 52
Robinson, Ava Marielle, 121, 142
Robinson, Marchel Jonery, 121, 141, 142

S
Smith, Durell Eugene, II., 121, 133
Smith, Michelle Denise Darden, 133
Smith, Quincy Rafael, 118, 129
Stevens, Valerie, 80
Sullivan, Bea, 128

T
Taipon, Elizabeth Ann, 129
Tomlin, Avery Robert Ricondo, 56, 57
Tomlin, Brooke Rose Irby, 53
Tomlin, Shirley Ann Irby-Robertson, 48, 49

W
Ware, Aaron, 161, 162
Ware, Edward, 162
Ware, Sandra, 162
Willis, Lisa, 82
Wilkinson, Michele Terese, 128
Worthy, Jermain Milton, III, 63
Worthy, Jermain Milton, Sr., 63
Worthy, Juda, 63
Wortz, Marla Colleen, Irby, 137, 138, 139
Wortz, Solomon, 137

Got an idea for a book? Contact Curry Brothers Books, LLC. We are not satisfied until your publishing dreams come true. We specialize in all genres of books, especially religion, leadership, family history, poetry, and children's literature. There is an African Proverb that confirms, *"When an elder dies, a library closes"*. Be careful who tells your family history. Are their values your family's values? Our staff will navigate you through the entire publishing process, and take pride in going the extra mile in meeting your publishing goals.

Improving the world one book at a time!

Curry Brothers Books, LLC
PO Box 247
Haymarket, VA 20168
(719) 466-7518 & (615) 347-9124
Visit us at www.currybrothersbooks.com

The Lord is my shepherd, I lack nothing.
He makes me lie down in green pastures,
he leads me beside quiet waters,
he refreshes my soul.
He guides me along the right paths
for his name's sake.
Even though I walk
through the darkest valley,
I will fear no evil,
for you are with me;
your rod and your staff,
they comfort me.
You prepare a table before me
in the presence of my enemies.
You anoint my head with oil;
my cup overflows.
Surely your goodness and love will follow me
all the days of my life,
and I will dwell in the house of the Lord forever.

Psalm 23

www.ingramcontent.com/pod-product-compliance
Lightning Source LLC
Chambersburg PA
CBHW042137290426
44110CB00002B/42